World-Famous mythologies

World-Famous

Author
Nemisharan Mital

PUSTAK MAHAL®

Publishers
Pustak Mahal®

Administrative office and sale centre
J-3/16 , Daryaganj, New Delhi-110002
☎ 23276539, 23272783, 23272784 • *Fax:* 011-23260518
E-mail: info@pustakmahal.com • *Website:* www.pustakmahal.com

Branches
Bengaluru: ☎ 080-22234025 • *Telefax:* 080-22240209
E-mail: pustak@airtelmail.in • pustak@sancharnet.in
Mumbai: ☎ 022-22010941, 022-22053387
E-mail: rapidex@bom5.vsnl.net.in
Patna: ☎ 0612-3294193 • *Telefax:* 0612-2302719
E-mail: rapidexptn@rediffmail.com

ISBN 978-81-223-0548-2

Edition: 2013

Printed at : Sharma Printers, Delhi.

PREFACE

Brought out with interesting, engrossing and authentic information, *World-Famous Mythologies* has long been popular with a wide array of readers. Tens of thousands of readers have boosted their knowledge of ancient facts through this book. Readers consider the book a mini-encyclopaedia in its own right when it comes to facts on mythology.

Mythologies on earth have arisen from numerous ancient cultures and civilisations and were subsequently enriched in the retelling over generations. These mythologies expressed belief and faith in the cosmic order and were a symbol of ancient human experience. All the mythologies helped create strong spiritual foundations in each culture.

Much before history was recorded, all ancient cultures had their own set of mythological beliefs and legends. These tales spoke of mighty celestial beings, gods, demons, evil spirits and witches, amongst others. In each and every tale, the constant battle between good and evil was depicted, with the ultimate triumph of good over evil being highlighted. The purpose of these legends was unmistakable: to foster a sense of ethics, compassion and human values in all people.

To compile innumerable tales into a single volume is an arduous task. But we have done our very best to present you with some of the model mythologies representing various cultures across the earth. There are 20 different mythologies in all, peppered with some rare illustrations.

It is our fond hope that, like previous editions of this book, the new crop of readers will also find *World-Famous Mythologies* a highly engrossing and enlightening read.

—Publishers

Contents

Introduction

A myth is a legend, a tale, a story, a saga of superhuman will, courage and strength handed down to a people by word of mouth over a long period of time, and put into written form by poets who made changes in the theme whenever it suited their purpose to do so.

Myths are supposed to be serious stories that reflect a society's spiritual foundations. They are symbols of human experience embodying a firm faith or belief in the cosmic view each culture holds dear to its heart and preserves tenaciously.

Mythology has tended to grow into theology, and myths tend to be viewed as the essence of religion. Myths are taken as conceived from a genuine religious experience. It is sacred experience that provides myths with their structure and converts them into beliefs. Famous psychologists like Carl Jung regard myths as the expression of a universal collective consciousness. Myths represent the response of people to life, the process of living, and their experience of the forces working about them.

Myths may also be viewed as pure fancy, the product of a race highly endowed with imagination and an artistic sense, which made them see beauty even in things which may be otherwise taken as ugly, and inclined to express their thoughts in the form of stories.

Myths are tales rather than historical accounts. But this fact does not minimise their importance and place in human life. Myths are felt and understood, and they play a dominant role in the development of our finer selves. Myths are an essential and priceless part of a culture and they are shared by men otherwise divided by artificial political barriers. For instance, countries as diverse as Egypt, Greece, Italy, France, Spain and Portugal share a number of myths. Similarly India, China, Japan, Thailand, Malaysia, Cambodia, Indonesia and Laos share their myths and beliefs.

Man, since times immemorial, has tried to find answer to a number of questions that arise in his mind about his personal identity, i.e. who am I, the nature of the universe, the power, force or reality behind the cosmic phenomena, his relationship with the universe and the Cosmic-Reality, his struggle for survival, his attitude towards death, and his equation with his family, community and human society at large.

Man has always felt that behind the physical phenomena there must be a hidden reality unalloyed by the gross matter and unaffected by the evils of decay and death. Myths represent this feeling and belief.

The Purpose of Myths

Myths have a serious purpose behind them. They are not just entertaining stories. Every major culture of the world has tried to explain the cosmic phenomenon, the powers behind the elements, beginnings of the universe and struggle for establishment of human and moral values, justice and benevolent social and politico-economic order in the universe through myths and mythological characters, gods and heroes.

Myths are not only an essential ingredient in a culture; they lay down a code of conduct for human beings, have an ethical bias, a normative tone and tenor, and they can be treated as the essence of a culture. They represent and set the character of a culture. Their basic purpose is to expose human weaknesses and to set models of human behaviour for their society.

One of the basic themes of myths has been an analysis of death and the netherworlds, resurrection or rebirth, and immortality. The gods have been raised to the level of immortality and the demons are condemned to the netherworld.

One of the purposes of myths has been to warn human beings against actions which would subject them to the wrath of gods. Almost all the major cultures have myths speaking of destruction through deluge.

Myths belonging to various cultures possess a basic unity and a common structure. The narrative content of a myth is not so important a part of it as the underlying structure. Myths reveal to us the basic reality that man, even in primitive stages of his technology, was master of a full-grown mind, and had the intellectual capacity to understand and interpret the world in which he lived, and the most important thing about him is that he was capable of relating to his environment and conditions of life--the world around him. ■■

Myths of Babylon - 1 : Marduk the Creator

The Babylonian civilization, though discovered as late as 1845, has been recognized as one of the earliest human civilizations on earth. During the course of their excavations at Nineveh, in what is now known as Iraq, the British archaeologists chanced to discover the library of Ashur Banipal, the Assyrian king. They were able to lay their hands upon a vast collection of clay tablets written upon in cuneiform script which, when deciphered, revealed the existence of a rich civilization. Amongst these tablets there are some inscribed with the myth of creation of the universe by the supreme god Marduk. Though the tablets date back to 1000 BC, there exists evidence which goes a long way to prove that Marduk was regarded the supreme deity as early as 1900 BC. In the introduction to his famous legal code, Hammurabi, who ruled over Babylon from 1782 BC to 1686 BC, refers to Marduk as "supreme among the gods ... king over all human beings."

According to the Babylonian mythology-in the beginning--there existed water only, the sweet waters and the salt waters. Mother-goddess Tiamat personified and ruled the salt waters and the Father--god Apsu personified and ruled sweet waters. Apsu and Tiamat happened to be the original gods - husband and wife. They had a son Mummu who existed in the mist that covered the water. Later Apsu and Tiamat produced another son Anshar and a daughter Kishar. Anshar married his sister Kishar who bore him a son, Anu, who in turn took his sister Nintu as his wife. Nintu gave birth to his two sons--Enlil and Ea--and two daughers--Ishtar (the goddess of love and war) and Damkina. Ea married his sister Damkina and became father of Marduk. Later Mother-goddess Tiamat produced--another son Kingu, and also created 11 monsters--the viper, the dragon, the sphinx, the lion, the mad dog, the scorpion man, three mighty storm demons, the dragon fly and the centaur.

Apsu Conspiracy

Tiamat and Apsu had become accustomed of living in peace which was now disturbed by their children, grandchildren and great grandchildren. They were too naughty and rowdy. Tiamat did not know how to control them, so she asked her husband Apsu to talk to them. But when Apsu tried to speak to them, they ignored him.

Apsu felt insulted. He decided to destroy his children. Tiamat did not agree with him and she advised Apsu to be more tolerant and understanding. But Mummu supported Apsu and they both entered into a consipiracy against the gods--Anshar, Kishar, Anu, Nintu, Enlil, Ea and Damkina. The unruly gods showed no respect for Apsu's authority and their behaviour destroyed Apsu's peace day and night. So Apsu decided to proceed with his plan to destroy them.

But before Apsu and Mummu could harm them, gods learnt about the sinister plot. Ea possessed magical powers through which he sensed the conspiracy hatched between the grand old man Apsu and his son Mummu. Every one of the various gods except Ea were terrified to hear of the plot. Ea, the wisest and the most accomplished among them, was prepared to undo the Apsu-Mummu conspiracy. He created a magic circle around the gods within which he lodged them securely. Then he cast a magic spell upon Apsu causing him to fall in deep slumber and made Mummu powerless in his face.

Ea's next step was to chain Apsu. He took away Apsu's crown and imperial halo,and placed them upon his own head. Having thus crowned himself, Ea killed Apsu, put a rope through Mummu's nose and led him away like an animal. Ea did not disturb Tiamat who ruled over salt waters. He established his rule over Apsu's body and the sweet waters. He married his sister Damkina and lived happily. In due course of time Damkina gave birth to their valiant son Marduk, who was born full-grown and was the wisest and ablest among all gods of three generations. Marduk was gifted with four sparkling eyes and four ears for him to see all and hear all. As he moved his lips, fire blazed from his mouth. He was extraordinarily tall and his limbs heavy and strong.

Marduk was taken as the Sun-god. He had the halo of ten suns around his head. Seeing him Anu, the grandfather of Marduk, decided to have Tiamat, her devil son Kingu and her demonic creatures finished. He created the four-fold winds flowing tempestuously in all the four directions and disturbing Kingu and his mother Tiamat of the salt waters. Kingu got enraged and he instigated Tiamat to avenge her husband's death upon gods and destroy them

Marduk, in direct combat with Tiamat.

forthwith. She agreed with Kingu and in order to destroy the gods, created 11 monsters and filled their bodies with deadly venom. Tiamat appointed Kingu as chief commander of her forces. Tiamat's forces were ready to tear at gods--none other than her own children who had rebelled against her and her husband.

Marduk Leads Gods

Ea came to know of Tiamat's plan to destroy the gods through his magical powers. He immediately went to his grandfather Anshar to inform him of the impending danger to his children. Anshar thought that Ea was quite capable of destroying the dragon-forces of Tiamat, his mother, and so he entrusted the job to Ea. But when Ea made a reconnaissance of Tiamat's monster army, he lost heart and informed Anshar that his magic would never measure upto the might of Tiamat's forces.

Then Anshar turned to his son Anu who, he thought, could resist and destroy Kingu's forces. Anu too found himself unequal to the task and told his father that he was not strong enough to carry out the assignment. At first, Anshar was disappointed, then his face began to glow and he asked his grandson Ea to bring his son to him.

He was confident that Marduk was quite capable of annihilating Tiamat and her forces led by Kingu.

Marduk appeared before his great-grandfather Anshar and assured him that he would surely carry out his assignment in letter and spirit and do away with Tiamat and her monsters. Anshar was happy to hear Marduk and he gave him his blessings.

But Marduk was a shrewd god. He decided to make the best use of the opportunity in order to enter into a deal with the gods. He asked Ansha, head of the assembly of gods, to give him a word that in case he was successful in conquering Tiamat and saving the lives of gods, he would be proclaimed supreme by the assembly of gods, his word would be final, his creation would remain abiding and he would be obeyed.

Anshar did not hesitate. He immediately issued orders for gods to assemble and to decree the supremacy of Marduk. The gods assembled. First they feasted upon bread and wine. Then they placed Marduk on a royal throne which they had built by themselves and proclaimed him the supreme god. They promised him obedience and made him king of the entire universe. Marduk was empowered to destroy, to create and to decide upon the fate of his subjects. He was adorned with royal robes, sceptre and the best of weapons. He was advised to spare the lives of all those who expressed their faith and trust in him instead of killing his opponents indiscriminately.

Marduk accepted the weapons handed to him by gods but he knew that those weapons would not be of much avail against the venomous creatures of Tiamat. He, therefore, made for himself a large bow and an arrow, hung the bow on his shoulder, took his mace and a net to ensnare Tiamat and a herb to undo the effect of poison the monster-dragons and serpents were sure to inject into his body during his fight against them.

Marduk invoked the seven terrific winds which stirred up the salty waters and enraged Tiamat. He let loose the mighty rain-storm and flooded the seas. When angry Tiamat came face to face with Marduk he took her to task for scheming against her own progeny and declaring Kingu as supreme god of the universe in a highly objectionable manner. Marduk challenged Tiamat to engage in a direct combat with him. Tiamat agreed. She stepped forward. Marduk immediately spread his net around her and as she opened her mouth wide in order to swallow Marduk, he made fierce winds blow into her mouth and expand her body. He picked up his bow and shot an arrow into her stomach which pierced through her heart and killed her.

Marduk fearlessly stood upon Tiamat's body and when Tiamat's monsters, seeing her dead, began to run helter-skelter, Marduk captured them and put them into his net. He crushed the bodies of the 11 monsters who stood by Tiamat's side, imprisoned Kingu and divested him of all the investitures of authority.

Cosmic Creation

After having conquered the enemy, Marduk engaged himself in cosmic creation. He stamped upon Tiamat's legs and crushed her skull with his mace. Then he tore Tiamat's body into two. With the upper half he created the sky and with the lower half the earth. He positioned Tiamat's head so as to create mountain, and from her eyes he made the two Mesopotamian rivers, Tigris and Euphrates, to flow.

Marduk appointed his grandfather Anu as ruler of the heavens, his father Ea as ruler of the earth, and Enlil to rule the air between the heaven and the earth. He created Sin (moon) and entrusted him the duty of illuminating nights. Sin's son Shamsh (Sun) was given days to illuminate.

Thereafter he ordered a huge temple to be built on the ground he had hardened for the gods to stay and be entertained with whenever they chose to visit earth, and he declared that his temple shall be called `the house of the great gods', i.e., Babylon. The temple was put under the charge of Ea. Then there arose the problem as to who would bring the gods their daily ration and serve them.

Marduk thereupon declared that he would collect blood and create bones from which he would create a savage to be called man. The job of man was prescribed to be the service of gods.

On the orders of Ea it was decided to kill the god responsible for instigating Tiamat for rebellion so that his blood could be used to form human beings. The assembly of gods unanimously declared that Kingu led the revolt. Then they bound him and presented him to Marduk and Ea. Ea killed Kingu, severed his blood vessels and created the first specimens of men out of Kingu's blood. Then Ea explained to the human beings thus created that the sole purpose of their lives was to serve the gods. ■■

Myths of Babylon - 2 : The Deluge

Myths of Babylon present a vivid description of the deluge--the great flood brought upon the land and the people of Babylonia by angry gods. The deluge-myth was for the fisrt time given a written form in 2100 BC. Gods had created human beings to offer them sacrifices and serve them. But with the passage of time the human beings became careless and negligent in the discharge of their duty towards gods. This made gods angry and they decided to distroy the human race and life as such on the earth.

Despite this decision, there were a few amongst gods who were directly responsible for and deeply involved in the creation of life and living beings, including men and women, on earth. These gods had developed filial affection for their creation and loved human beings as their own children. They, therefore, were not mentally prepared for the total destruction of the seed of plants and trees, animals and birds, grains and fruits, and the righteous amongst men well-versed in the crafts of life. It is this theme around which the following Deluge-Myth has been woven.

In ancient Messopotamia there was the famous city of Shuruppak, the capital of Sumer, where gods and men lived together on the banks of the river Euphrates. Gods lived in their hallowed and magnificent temples and human beings in their homes. When men and gods both became old, Enlil, the ruler of the gods, called the gods together in assembly, and complained that the human beings who lived upon earth had become numerous beyond count, and that they are too noisy. The earth bellows like a herd of wild oxen. The clamour of human beings disturbs me in my sleep.

Enlil's complaint against human beings was similar to Tiamat's complaint against her children--the gods. Enlil, like Apsu, decided to destroy the human race together. In order to achieve this objective, he asked the rain-god Adad to cause heavy rains to pour down upon the earth throughout the day and night for several days to let loose a great flood upon earth which should drown the dwellers of Shuruppak. Goddess Ishtar seconded the proposal placed by Enlil before the assembly, and all other gods, except Ea, expressed agreement with the plan. Ea sat silently because in his heart he did not approve of the plan to destroy life and the means to life which he had created so laboriously. Ea loved human beings and thought of a plan to save the seed of life on earth. By his magical powers, he presented himself before Utanapishtim, king of Shuruppak, and asked him to stand by the wall of his reed-hut in order to listen to what Ea had to tell him. He wanted to entrust Utanapishtim with a secret task which he was asked to carry out in strict confidence and obedience.

When Utanapishtim got close to the reed-wall, he heard Ea's voice. Ea told him that Shuruppak was going to be overwhelmed and destroyed by a flood of very high magnitude by the command of Enlil and the consent of gods. Ea asked Utanapishtim to save his life and in order to do that he advised him to dismantle his house and construct, with its timber, a huge boat in ark shape equal in length and breadth. Ea wanted Utanapishtim to build his ship of solid timber to ward off the rays of sun (Shamsh) and to seal it carefully so that the water might not seep into the ship. He was advised to take aboard his wife, his relatives, craftsmen of the city, all sorts of grains, seeds of all living things and animals and birds. Ea promised to give a signal for the king to seal the entry of the ship. At the king's request Ea made a drawing of the ark on the ground for him to copy.

Then the king asked the lord Ea: "...When the people of Shuruppak ask me what I am doing, how shall I respond?" Ea replied to him: "..... Tell them, `I have learned that Enlil hates me so that I can no longer live in your city, nor can I place my feet anywhere in that gods' territory. Therefore I will go down to the deep and live with my lord Ea. However, Enlil intends to shower you with abundance. After a stormy evening you will find unusual birds and fish, and your land will be filled with rich harvests."

Shuruppak craftsmen took full five days to construct the ship. It was 200 feet long, 200 feet wide and 200 feet high, and its floor space measured about an acre. In the interior of the ship, the king made seven floors, and each floor was divided into nine sections. The ship was thoroughly sealed on the sixth day and on the seventh day it was moved into the water of the river Euphrates. Then the king took aboard his family, his relatives, the choicest craftsmen and also the seeds of all living things, grasses and grains. As soon as god Adad caused the heavens to darken with terrible storm clouds on

Utanapishtim's ship floating on the deluge-waters.

instructions from Shamsh, the king boarded the ship and sealed the entrance. The ship was then left to drift in the deluge-waters at the mercy of the raging storm.

The cosmos was plunged into darkness and the people of Shuruppak, along with all other living beings, were completely overwhelmed and destroyed by the raging waters. When the goddess Ishtar saw the wholesale destruction upon earth, she cried and lamented for consenting to Enlil's proposal to seek destruction of a world she had created and loved so much. Ishtar was not alone; the enormity of destruction made all the gods other than Enlil realize that they had committed a blunder in lending their consent to the destruction. They all wept along with Ishtar for what they had wrought. The deluge lasted for seven days and seven nights consecutively. The windstorm tossed Utanapishtim's giant ship wildly upon the raging flood waters. The flood-bearing south wind slackened on the eighth day and the turbulent waters became calm. The sun shone once again brightly in the sky making the entire scene of

Goddess Istar, who repented later upon the destruction of her own creation.

destruction visible of gods. Utanapishtim's ship became steady upon the water. Assured of cessation of the hostile winds, the king opened a window on the topmost floor of his seven story ship-house and looked in vain for a coastline. Earth was completely submerged under a vast sheet of flood waters and, but for the living beings aboard his ship, there was no sign of life anywhere around.

When the first rays of Shams (Sun) fell upon the face of the king, he knelt in reverence for the mighty sun and paid his obeisance to gods. He took an ox and a sheep out of the livestock he had preserved upon the ship and sacrificed them to gods. Utanapishtim could not bear the sight of the destruction of life upon earth. He sat down and tears began rolling down his cheeks. He was unable to locate the spot where his ship happened to be at the moment as all the mountain tops were totally submerged under the water for another twelve days. On the twelfth day, when he opened the window once again, he found his ship anchored on the top of the Mount Nisir. The ship remained there for next seven days as if chained to the mountain top. On the seventh day, the king set a dove free into the sky. The dove flew for a while and then returned to the ship as it could not find a place to alight upon and rest.

After some time Utanapishtim offered food and drink to gods on top of the Mount Nisir. The gods gathered around the king in no time. The king prostrated before Anu and Enlil. Ishtar was extremely glad to find that the king had saved some of her creation. She mourned the dead and cursed Enlil for the destruction wrought by him. Enlil, on the contrary, was enraged to see the king and his ship which had survived the deluge. He called for an explanation from the gods as to who had permitted escape of the king and all those who were safely aboard the ship against his specific command that the flood should not leave a trace of life on earth.

Ea, then, came forward and told Enlil that the flood was caused to punish the sinners and the guilty, but punishment does not mean indiscriminate annihilation. Ea also told Enlil that he had nothing to do with Utanapishtim's escape. As a matter of fact, Utanapishtim had a dream in which he was warned of the impending disaster and told how to escape and survive the flood. On hearing this, Enlil surmised that Utanapishtim must have been a pure soul to have the dream and survive the food. So he took the king and his wife by hand into the ship and blessed them. He granted them eternal life and praised them for the preservation of the seeds of humanity as also the seeds of plant and animal lives.

Enlil permitted Utanapishtim to reestablish his kingdom at Shuruppak to resettle the human beings he had saved in his ship in the city and to make the earth bustle with life once again. Utanapishtim bowed to the gods and life returned to earth once again because of a just and benevolent king who loved his land and his people. ■■

Myths of China - 1 : Chang Tao-ling

Chang Tao-ling has become an inseparable part of Chinese mythology. He is supposed to be a close disciple of the legendary philosopher-saint-poet of China, Lao Tzu, who is said to have handed over a mystic treatise to Chang Tao-ling. By following the instructions given in the treatise, he was successful in his search of the elixir of life. One day, when he was preparing the elixir, a spiritual being appeared before him and revealed to him that in a stone-house on the mountain Po-sung were concealed certain ancient works which could teach him the art of ascending to Heaven.

Chang Tao-ling found those works and by means of them obtained the powers of flying in the sky, hearing distant sounds and wandering in the world and the Heaven leaving his body behind to return to it at will. He was guided in his supernatural practices by a goddess and he had succeeded in conquering demons and natural forces like the wind and the thunder.

One day he told his disciples that on the seventh day of the moon a man would come from the east, and there arrived a man on the appointed day, named Chao Sheng, who later became famous as his chief disciple. After his arrival Chang Tao-ling took his flock to the highest peak of the mountain Yun-t' ai below which there was a peach tree. Chang dared his disciples to gather the frut of the tree and promised to communicate a spiritual formula (mantra) to the successful one. None except Chao Sheng dared to perform the feat. Chao Sheng successfully reached the tree, gathered the fruit and threw the peaches one by one up to Chang Tao-ling, but he found it hard to ascend back to the mountain top. Chao Sheng was thirty feet below the mountain top, and when Chang Tao-ling extended his arm for Chao Sheng to hold and rise to the top, Chang's disciples were overawed at the miraculous powers of the master.

One day Chang Tao-ling was on the mountain Ho- ming Shan, accompanied by his disciple Wang Ch'ang. There he saw a shaft of white light. He pointed toward that shaft of light on the distant

Chang Tao-ling, an inseperable part of Chinese mythology

Yang Shan top and told Wang that some evil spirits infested the place. He took Wang along with him and walked down to the foothill where they met twelve women who were none else but the evil spirits. Chang Tao-ling asked them about the source of the white shaft of light. They answered that the white shaft of light was nothing else but the 'Yin', the female principle of the universe. Then Chang Tao-ling felt the presence of salt water in the vicinity of the place where he stood with the evil spirits. He asked the spirits about the source of the salt water. The spirits pointed to a pond in front of him in which, they told him, lived a poisonous dragon. Chang tried his best to force the dragon out of the pond, but he failed in the first attempt. Then he drew a phoenix with golden wings and hurled it into the air over the pond. This frightened the dragon and dried up the pond in a moment's time. Chang Tao-ling did not kill the dragon but let it escape. Then he took out his sword from the sheath and stuck it in the ground causing a salt water well to be formed on the spot.

The evil spirits, thereupon, bowed to Chang and each one of them presented a jade ring to him. Chang Tao-ling took all the twelve rings into his hand, pressed them and forged them into a single large ring. While presenting him with a ring each one of the evil spirits had expressed a desire to become his wife.

Chang Tao-ling took the large ring he had forged in his hand and threw it into the salt-water well. Then he told the women that whoever of them recovered the ring from the well should be his wife. Actually he had adopted this trick to drown all of them in the well. One by one each one of them descended into the well and none could emerge from it what to say of recovering the ring. The evil spirits were thus destroyed by Chang. He gave them a new identity, "Spirits of the Well"

Chang then prepared to leave the place, but before he could do so a hunter reached there. Chang exhorted the hunter to give up the evil profession of killing the living beings to earn his living. Thereupon the hunter asked Chang to prescribe an alternative profession to him. He was very pleased to hear the hunter and asked him to draw salt-water from the well and retrieve salt from it. The hunter accepted Chang's advice and gave up hunting.

The people of the surrounding area soon realized how the visit of Chang Tao-ling had helped them. Their cattle was protected from the dragon and the hunter, they were no more afraid of the evil spirits, and they were able to obtain salt. The hunter too realized that Chang's advice had provided him with a more honourable profession. They all joined together in dedicating the territory, known as Ling Chou, to Chang Tao-ling and built a temple to commemorate his visit to the area and to offer him sacrifices.

The name of Chang Tao-ling is a household word in China even today and it wields immense spiritual power throughout the land. ■■

Myths of China - 2 : Chiang Tzu-ya

Chiang Tzu-ya is one of the mythological canonized generalissimos of China. He is regarded as the most influential celestial generalissimo in the wars which led to the overthrow of the legendary tyrant Chou Wang and his dynasty and the establishment of the great Chou dynasty. The decisive epic battle took place in 1122 BC, which destroyed Chou Wang in his palace fire and won the title of Father and Counsellor for Chiang Tzu-ya from Wu Wang.

Chiang Tzu-ya was devoutly spiritual in his outlook and received divine wisdom which helped him act in the righteous manner. In the midst of war once he went to visit the K'un-lun mountain in his spirit chariot. On his arrival at the Unicorn Precipice he was lost in the loverly natural beauty. From there he went to visit the Jade Palace of Abstraction where he was presented to the enlightened Yuan-Shih, the son and avatar of P'an Ku, the mythical being who created universe out of chaos for the first time. Yuan-Shih was treated as highest in the heaven and the god of lightning. He gave the list of `Promotions to Immortals' to Tzu-Ya and asked him to erect a holy terrace and exhibit the list there. Yuan-Shih also warned him that if any one called him on his way he had to take care not to answer the call.

Yuan-Shih was a god. He had foreseen the events. On his return journey Tzu-ya was thrice called by his old classmate Shen Kung-pao in the Jade Palace of Abstraction. Shen Kung-pao tried to convince him of the superiority of magical arts over abstract spiritualism. He boasted of his magical powers and told him that he could take off his own head, hurl it into the space, bring it back from there and fix it back on his neck and be a normal person once again. He despised immortality and advised Tzu-ya to throw away the List of Immortals and join him. Tzu-ya promised to burn the list provided that Kung-pao demonstrated his skill at severing his head from his neck and refixing it.

Shen Kung-pao made a perfect demonstration of cutting his

Tree of wealth: People in China believe–when God of riches, Chao Kung-ming, listens the prayers, Tree of wealth springs up in their homes.

head with a sword he held in the right hand and hurling it into space. The presiding deity and Ancient Immortal of the South Pole, who had been keeping a track of Tzu-ya's movements, witnessed the scene Shen Kung-pao had presented before Tzu-ya. He immediately despatched one of his immortals to assume the form of a crane and fetch Shen Kung-pao's head in its beak.

Tzu-ya was amazed at the feat performed by Shen Kung-pao. He was looking upwards when he realized that someone had pulled him from behind. He turned and found the Ancient Immortal, Hsien-weng, standing behind him. Tzu-ya asked Hsien-weng why he had taken the trouble of visiting him. Hsien-weng told him that he had to follow him because of his violation of the instructions given him by Yuan-Shih and his promise to burn the list. He also told Tzu-ya that it was at his orders that the crane had taken away Shen Kung-

Wen Chung, the minister of thunder, whom Chian Tzu-ya defeated.

pao's head which would not be returned to him. He also wanted him that the would have to die because if the head is not replanted on his neck within an hour and three quarters, the blood circulation would stop and thereafter replanting the head would not be possible. In doing this, Hsien-weng wanted to teach Shen a lesson that the magical arts are incapable of raising human soul to the level of immortality.

Tzu-ya became concerned about Shen's life and he persuaded Hsien-weng to restore Shen's head to him within one hour and three quarters so that he may live. Shen was also getting anxious. In the meantime, Hsien-weng signalled to the crane to drop Shen Kung-pao's head upon his neck. The head fell facing backward but Shen Kung-pao turned it round by his ear. He opened his eyes and saw Hsien-weng before him who scolded him for his charlatanry. Shen Kung-pao hanged his head in shame and mounting his tiger he made off.

The crane with Shen Kung Pao's head, flying high in the sky; watching from the ground: Chiang Tzu-ya and Hsien-weng.

In another battle Chiang Tzu-ya defeated Wen Chung, the minister of thunder, with the help of immortals. Chiang Tzu-ya was well versed in witchcraft. Once Chao Kung-ming, a hermit on Mount O-mei, decided to fight against Tzu-ya. Tzu-ya was not willing to face the master of considerable spiritual powers with weapons. He made a straw image of him, wrote his name on it, burned incense and worshipped it for twenty days, and on the twenty first day shot arrows made of peachwood into its eyes and heart. At the same moment Kung-ming fell ill, fainted and died. Later Chiang Tzu-ya secured release of his spirit along with the spirits of other heroes from the netherworld. When the spirit of Chao Kung-ming was led into his presence he admitted that he was killed through foul means and raised him to the august office of President of the Ministry of Riches and Prosperity in the government of gods.

The God of riches is even now worshipped in China. This

much-adored deity causes trees of money to grow from which cash may be obtained simply by shaking its branches. He also has a magical casket full of gold and silver which never gets exhausted.

Chiang Tzu-ya became Prime Minister in the divine government. He conferred twenty eight constellations upon his followers on which they all settled down as immortals. Chiang also canonized Yin Chiao who was born to Queen Chiang of the Emperor Chou. At the time of his birth he looked like a lump of formless flesh. Ta Chi, the infamous concubine, saw Yin Chiao as an opportunity to take her revenge upon the queen and she reported to the king that the queen had given birth to a demon. The king immediately ordered the child to be thrown out. He also ordered the queen to be thrown down from an upper story of the palace and killed under the plea that the queen could not have given birth to a demon unless she had not been unfaithful to the king and sleeping with an evil monster.

Chiang Tzu-ya was pleased with Yin Chiao for the reason that as he grew up under the care of Shen Chen-jen, who had picked him from the wayside and brought him up, Yin Chiao avenged his mother's murder by fighting against the unjust king and killed Ta Chi. Chiang Tzu-ya held all those in high regard who did their duty towards their wronged parent or parents.

Chiang Tzu-ya is regarded as a powerful and respectful god among the Chinese pantheon. ■■

Myths of China - 3 : Miao Shan

In ancient times China was divided into a number of small states. In western China, there was the state of Hsing Lin quite close to India. It had Miao Chuang as its king. The king had lived nearly half a century without having any male issue to succeed to the throne. This was a great source of grief to the king and his queen Pao Te. At the request of the king and the queen, fifty Buddhist and Tao priests prayed for seven days and seven nights before the God of Hua Shan, the sacred mountain in the west, and they offered rare and valuable presents. On the eighth day the king and the queen personally offered prayers and sacrifices to the god of the sacred mountain. But the god of Hua Shan was aware that the king had been deprived of a male heir as a punishment for the blood he had shed in his fight against the rightful rulers of the state which he had usurped. The god, however, could not altogether reject his prayer as the priests had interceded for him and the king had come in person to offer the sacrifices. The king was told that soon he would have children. But the god had secretly decided to grant him three daughters only, and no son.

After exactly nine months the queen gave birth to a daughter. She was named Miao Ching. A year went by, and another daughter was born. She was named Miao Yin. And, at the end of the third year, yet another daughter was born who was named Miao Shan. When the king heard about the birth of the third daughter, he was quite desperate and enraged. He was past fifty and had no male child and his dynasty was bound to become extinct for the lack of a heir.

King Miao Chuang's learned minister tried to console him saying, "Heaven has granted you three daughters. When they grow up, we will choose three sons-in-law for your majesty and you can elect your successor from among them."

In course of time, the king's third daughter Miao Shan became known for her modesty and numerous other good qualities. She observed all the tenets and rituals of the Buddhist religion. Her life-conduct was highly virtuous. One day, when the three sisters were playing in the palace garden of Perpetual Spring, Miao Shan told her sisters: "Riches and glory are like the rain in spring or the morning dew: a little while and soon all is over. Kings and emperors expect to enjoy to the end the good fortune they possessed, but sickness lays them low in their graves and then all is over. Where are now all those powerful dynasties which have laid down the law to the world? As for me, I desire nothing more than a retreat on a mountain in order to attain perfection. If I succeed in the attainment of perfection, then, borne on the clouds of heaven, I will travel throughout the universe passing in the twinkling of an eye from east to west. I will rescue my parents from the worldly afflictions and take them to heaven. I will protect the miserable and afflicted people of the world. I will transform the hearts of evil-doers and engage them in noble tasks. This is what I yearn for"

Miao Shan had hardly finished speaking when a lady of the royal court announced to the sisters that the king had selected spouses for his two elder daughters and the wedding was fixed for the next day. The lady requested them to be quick and get ready with their wedding dresses and presents. The king's order was binding.

The king had chosen an academician Chao Kuei, son of one of his ministers, for the eldest one Miao Ching, and a military officer Chao Yang for the second daughter Miao Yin. The marriage ceremonies had been planned on a grand scale.

Miao Shan's Decision

It was now Miao Shan's turn. Her parents were in search of an able spouse for her worthy of succeeding to the throne. The king summoned Miao Shan to his presence and conveyed his plans about her to the girl. The king also told her that all his hopes rested on her.

Miao Shan spoke quite humbly, "I regard it a crime to disobey my father. I beg your pardon if my views differ from yours. I wish to remain unmarried and attempt to attain perfection and Buddhahood. I assure you that I shall ever remain grateful to you."

The king was enraged to hear his daughter and he cried, "You, a wretched girl! You think you can teach me, the ruler of a great people and head of a state. Have you ever seen a princess become a nun? Can there be a noble woman amongst the nuns? Set aside all these nonsensical ideas and tell me if you would marry a first-rate academician or a military officer."

Miao Shan replied, "Who doesn't love royal dignity and who doesn't like happiness in marriage? However, I would love to be a nun alone. I don't feel the least attraction for the worldly glory and riches. My only ambition is to make my mind pure and purer still."

The angry king rose to throw her out of his presence. Miao Shan knew that to defy her father openly was an impossible thing, so she thought of an alternative and said, "If I am not allowed to remain unwed, I would choose to marry a physician." This further infuriated the king and he wondered if his realm was wanting in young men from aristocratic families and the talented ones.

Miao Shan was undaunting. She told her father plainly that she wanted to heal humanity of all its ills--cold, heat, lust, old age and all kinds of infirmities. I would have all the social classes treated on the ground of equality, the poor and rich held on equal footing without distinction between man and man.

The king lost his temper and cried angrily, "You wicked imbecile! How dare you to place such diabolical suggestions before me?" He was not prepared to hear further arguments. Summoning his palace guard, he said, "This wretched nun is bent upon insulting me. Let her take off her royal robes and leave her in the Queen's garden to perish of cold. That will remove one cause of worry to my mind."

Miao Shan fell on her knees and thanked her father for his orders. She devoted herself to the attainment of Nirvana in the Queen's garden. She could not be dissuaded by anyone from the path she had chosen for herself. The king ultimately permitted her to join the nunnery with strict orders that the nuns already there would make their best effort to dissuade the princess from following the path of renunciation.

But Miao Shan would not budge from her resolve to attain perfection. The superior nun did not know how to deal with Miao Shan. In order to break her, she entrusted the entire responsibility of running the nunnery kitchen upon her single-handed. She told Miao Shan that if even a single nun at the nunnery felt displeased with her management of the kitchen and the food she served there, she would be turned away. Miao Shan undertook the task silently and went to pray before Buddha-'Ju Lai'. She knelt before him and prayed: "O Great Buddha! O thou merciful and generous Lord! This humble servant of yours wishes to give up the worldly connections. Grant my prayer. May I never yield to the temptations offered to divert me from my path." And, thereafter, Miao Shan promised to observe the rules and regulations of the nunnery and to obey her superiors over there.

It was really a tough job for a princess to carry out all the tasks of the kitchen single-handed but she devoted herself to them in the right earnest. Seeing this Yu Huang, the Master of Heaven, ordered his powers to assist Miao Shan in the discharge of her functions. The Superior Nun was astonished to find that the divinity Chieh Lan cleaned the kitchen, the sea-dragon dug a well near the kitchen and supplied the kitchen with water, a tiger brought firewood from the forest, the fire-god lit the kitchen fire and put it out after the food was cooked, the birds from heaven collected vegetables from fields and brought them to Miao Shan's kitchen, and the nunnery bell boomed of itself every evening at dusk as if struck by some mysterious hand.

Impressed by all these miracles, the Superior Nun sent for the king with the request that he better recall his daughter respectfully to the royal palace because she happened to be a realized soul.

The message sent the king into rage. He ordered one of his military generals to take with him a contingent of 500 infantry and cavalry, surround the nunnery and burn it to ground together with the nuns. The general carried out his mission. When the nuns saw the nunnery on fire and all escape routes sealed by the king's men, they became frightened and remarked to Miao Shan contemptuously, "It is you who has brought this terrible disaster upon us."

Miao Shan admitted quite humbly that the lives of 500 odd nuns were under threat of destruction only because of her. She knelt down and prayed to Buddha: "O Great Sovereign of the Earth! Your servant is the daughter of King Miao Chuang while you are the son of king Shuddhodhana. Will you not rescue your younger sister? You have left your palace, I have left mine. You in former times betook to solitary confinement to attain perfection, I came here with the same object. Will you not save us from this fiery destruction?"

Having prayed thus, Miao Shan took a bamboo pin from her hair, pricked the roof of her mouth with it and spat the flowing blood toward heaven. Immediately, the clear sky was covered with dark clouds on all sides and it rained heavily. The rain water put out the fire. The nuns expressed their gratitude towards Miao Shan, kneeling before her and thanking her effusively for having saved their lives.

The king's general retreated to the capital hastily and informed the king about the extraordinary powers of his daughter. The king was still more furious and he ordered Miao Shan's arrest. He wanted her brought to him in chains and beheaded. The queen thought that Miao Shan could still be persuaded to give up her path. She requested the king to allow her to have a grand pavilion built at the side of the road the chained Miao Shan was to pass through while being taken to the execution ground. The queen told the king that she would go to the pavilion along with her two remaining daughters and their husbands to participate in a programme of music, dance and feasting in order to impress upon Miao Shan that she had only made her life miserable. The queen thought Miao Shan would surely take the hint seeing them merry-making.

The king agreed to have Miao Shan's execution stayed till the queen's preparations were completed. But the queen's plan failed miserably. When Miao Shan saw her mother and sisters engaged in festivities in the pavilion on her way to the execution ground, she was not in the least impressed and she let it be known to her mother in clear terms that she had no love for pomp and show. She said, "I swear that I prefer death to the socalled joys of the world."

Miao Shan was then led to the execution ground. The king-in-court was present to witness her beheading. Miao Shan was taken as dead and ritual sacrifices were made to her. A priest recited the oration as a part of her last rites.

At this point the queen arrived there and ordered the officials to return to their posts. On finding her daughter alone, the queen tried her best to bring her to the king's point of view, but Miao Shan listened to her mother's discourse in silence with bent head and in disdain. The king too did not want to shed his daughter's blood. He ordered her to be kept in the royal palace as a prisoner so that he could make a last effort to persuade her to change her ways. The king did his best but Miao Shan would not relent. The king then decided to have her decapitated on the next day.

The next day Miao Shan was led to the place of execution. She stood erect and said, "Today I give up this world for the attainment of a more perfect life. Hurry up, take my life, but desist from mutilating my body."

The Last Journey

The executioners received the king's orders and prepared to execute her. All of a sudden the sky became overcast with dark clouds. It was dark all around, only Miao Shan's face was surrounded by a halo. She looked cheerful and bright. The executioner's sword fell upon Miao Shan's neck and instead of hurting her, it broke into two. The executioner picked up his spear. It too broke into pieces. The king then ordered her to be strangled with a silk cord. The device worked. As soon as Miao Shan breathed her last, a tiger leapt into the execution ground, placed her body on his back and disappeared into the pine forest. The king was informed about the incident.

Miao Shan's dead body was then preserved by the gods in a secluded place. They put a magic pill into her mouth in order to arrest decay and disintegration of her physical remains so that it remained in perfect condition for her soul to reenter it and resume life once again.

Death meant inanimation of the body alone as it left the soul unhurt and intact. Miao Shan's soul was borne by gods on clouds who took her to a secluded place where she recovered her consciousness and signed: "My father had me strangled. How have I reached this place? How can I live in this desolate and lonely region?" While she was still musing like this, a young man dressed in blue and shining garments appeared with a large banner and said to her, "I come to take you to the ten infernal regions by order of Yen Wang, the king of the Hells."

Miao Shan asked the young man, "What is this cursed place where I am now?" He told her that they were in the netherworld Hell and gods of the ten Hells were impressed and pleased at her sacrifice. He asked her to follow him fearlessly.

Thus Miao Shan began her visit to the ten infernal regions. On her way she was greeted by the gods of the ten Hells. Miao Shan, seeing them bowing to her, told them that she was not a great person for them to show her respect and regard. The gods replied, "We have heard that when you pray, all evil disappears instantly. We want to hear you pray." Miao Shan agreed on the condition that all the souls held prisoner in all the ten Hells were released from the

Miao Shan, who sacrificed everything to attain perfection and Buddhahood, riding the tiger that carries her to the sacred mountain Hsian Shan.

chains that bound them and brought into her presence to hear her pray.

The condition was met forthwith. No sooner had Miao Shan finished her prayers than the Hell was transformed into paradise and the instruments of torture into lotus-flowers. Seeing this Pan Kuan, the registrar of the Hells, pleaded before Yen Wang, the king of the Hell, that according to the divine dispensation existence of both Heaven and Hell was imperative, but because of Miao Shan's admission to the Hell, the Hell had been transformed into paradise. It was, therefore, essential to do something about it.

Yen Wang decreed, "Pan Kuan is right. Let, therefore, forty-eight flag-bearers escort Miao Shan from the gate of the Hell to the pine forest so that she may reenter her body and resume her life in the upper world". The decree was carried out and Miao Shan awakened in her body as if from a dream.

Buddha's Appearance

As soon as Miao Shan's body came back to life, Ju Lai Buddha appeared before her incognito and asked her, "Why have you come to this place?" Miao Shan narrated the tale of her woes before the visitor without knowing who he was. Buddha said, "I greatly pity your misfortune, but there is no one to assist you here. I too am alone in this vast world. If you agree, we can enter into marriage, build a hut for ourselves and live in peace."

Miao Shan was not prepared to hear all that. She replied, "You should not make such an impossible suggestion to me. I sacrificed my life to keep the vow of virginity, and you are talking to me in such a light vein! You may please leave me alone."

Buddha was highly pleased to hear her. Having decided to reveal his identity, he said, "Miao Shan, I am pleased to hear you say that. I am no other than the Buddha you are seeking. I was testing your virtue and I am highly satisfied with you. This place is not suitable for you to conduct your ascetic pursuits. I invite you to the Hsing Shan--the sacred mountain."

Miao Shan was thrilled to see the Master before her. She fell on her knees, paid her obeisance to him and said, "My Master, my eyes have deceived me. I never expected you at this desolate place. Pardon me for my seeming disrespect foward your Holiness." She then asked Buddha where the Hsiang Shan happened to be located, and she was frightened to hear that the mountain was far away. Realising the cause of her fear, Buddha gave her a divine peach fruit and assured her that after she had eaten it, she would experience neither hunger, thirst and old age nor death and that she would become immortal.

Miao Shan ate the divine peach, took leave of Ju Lai Buddha and started upon her journey toward Hsiang Shan. She had hardly taken half a dozen steps when a tiger appeared in the middle of the road roaring loudly. Miao Shan said to the tiger, "I am a poor girl deprived of filial affection and piety. I disobeyed my father. I beseech you to devour me and thus put an end to my life."

The tiger replied, "I am guardian of the boundaries of Hsiang Shan. I have been sent here to carry you. Please get on my back. I will take you to the shrine."

Miao Shan reached Hsiang Shan in no time. She attained her goal--perfection and Buddhahood--after nine years of hard ascetic practices on that holy retreat. Since then Miao Shan has undertaken the task of relieving the misery of all those who invoke her help. ■■

Egyptian Mythology : Osiris

Egyptian civilization was in full bloom in 4000 BC. It was deeply religious from the beginning. It had faith in divinity as well as in the divine content of man. One of its major beliefs was the continuity of life after death. Egyptian civilization believed that life did not end with death and that the dead person continued to live in another world--the netherworld--where he received treatment according to the quality of his actions during his life on earth. If his heart was pure and his actions noble, he was well entertained in the life after death and, conversely, if his heart was impure and actions ignoble, he was given a scornful treatment. This was the reason why the Egyptians neither buried their dead in graves nor cremated their bodies. They preserved them in mummies and kept them well provided for in pyramids.

Atum or Re--the sun god--was the supreme Egyptian deity, the supreme God. Re produced Shu, god of air, and Tefnut, goddess of moisture. Shu and Tefnut were the primeval pair who, in turn, brought forth Geb, the earth god and Nut, the sky goddess. Here the Egyptian mythology takes a curious turn.

Re Weds Nut

Nut, the sky goddess, was extremely good, beautiful and kind. Re took fancy for her and married her. Re created the universe. By using magical powers, he also created Thoth, the lord of divine wisdom in order to give law to the universe and lay down cardinal principles of justice and order.

Although Nut was married to Re, she had a natural feeling for her brother Geb, lord of the earth, and she developed tender feelings and love for Thoth also. When Re discovered that Nut had secretly slept with Geb, he was enraged at her and cursed her that she would not be able to give birth to the child she carried in her womb in any month of the year. Nut was terrified at the curse. She went to her lover Thoth with tears in her eyes and sought his help. She told Thoth that of the five children she was carrying one was his.

Thoth, the lord of divine-wisdom who has created the five additional days of the solar year to rescue Nut from Re's curse.

Thoth spoke to her gentle and affectionate words and assured her that Re's curse would be rendered ineffective and she would become the Mother of Gods before the next year began.

Thoth's problem was to find five days for the birth of Nut's five children beyond the twelve months, i.e. 360 days of the solar year Re had fashioned. He, therefore, decided to approach Moon. It should be recalled here that Thoth is supposed to be the rescuer and guardian of Moon.

Thoth knew that Moon loved to play games, so he invited Moon to play games with him on the condition that every time Thoth won the game, Moon would give him a little of his light. Moon had no objection. During the next few months Thoth and Moon played games and Thoth saved the illumination he received from Moon every time he won the game. Finally, when he had enough illumination to make five full days, he stopped playing with

Moon and returned to Nut to help her give birth to her five children on the five days he had been able to add to the 360 days of Re's solar year.

On the first day Nut gave birth to Osiris, the son of her husband Re. As soon as Osiris was born the heavens proclaimed: "The good and great King Osiris, lord of all the earth, has been born." On the next day another of Re's sons, Horus the Elder, was born.

Nut delivered her brother's (Geb's) son Seth on the third day. In fact Seth had himself chosen the day and the extraordinary manner of his birth. He cut an opening into his mother's side and forced his way into the world. On the fourth day Nut delivered the Great Goddess Isis, the daughter of Thoth, the master of words and law-giver of the universe. And, on the fifth day Nephthys, the daughter of Geb, was born.

Re's son Osiris and Thoth's daughter Isis loved each other from the time they shared their mother's womb. When they grew up, they got married to each other. Seth married his sister Nephthys. Despite the fact that Nephthys married Seth, the worst enemy of Osiris, she always loved her sister Isis and her brother Osiris and helped them in hard times.

In due course of time Osiris became the king of Upper and Lower Egypt. The reign of Osiris was a golden age, the model for subsequent generations. He taught the arts of civilization to his subjects. A New Kingdom hymn says :

> "He .... established justice throughout both banks (of the Nile), he put the sun in his father's place .... overthrowing the adversary with might and power.... (The people) saw how excellent he was and entrusted the kingdom to him to lead the two lands into prosperity."

Thus Osiris took charge of the people who were leading a nomadic life. He taught them the art of farming and settled them. He also gave them laws and established peace and order on earth.

The Conspiracy

After teaching his people the lessons of civilized life, Osiris travelled to other parts of the earth to spread his ideas. In his absence his younger brother Seth, who was jealous of Osiris, conspired to overthrow and kill him. He was able to enlist the support of 72 Egyptians to his cause.

Osiris, whose period of reign was considered as Golden Age of the ancient Egypt.

After Osiris returned from foreign lands, Seth plotted to have him shut in a box and disposed of. One night, when Osiris was fast asleep in his bed, Seth secretly measured his body. The next day he summoned his favourite craftsmen and commanded them to prepare a box of wood strictly according to the measurements (of Osiris' body) which he handed to them. When the box was ready, the best of the land's artists were entrusted with the task of decorating it. The assignment was carried out with care and refinement. The box looked like a piece of finest craftsmanship and decor.

One day Seth threw a gala party to which Osiris was especially invited. The other invitees were 72 co-conspirators of Seth. Osiris attended the party quite unaware of his brother's intentions. He did not take even a single bodyguard with him.

After the meals and the entertainment were over, Seth gave a signal to his attendants to bring the box into the hall. The box was admired by his guests. Seth took this opportunity to throw a bet. He promised to offer the box to one of his invitees whose body properly fitted the box on climbing into it. One by one Seth's co-conspirators climbed into it but none of them had a body that would fit into the box. Then the final moment came for Seth's sinister game to succeed. Osiris, unaware of Seth's plot, climbed into it and as he lay in the box his body fitted so well into it that before he could lift it out of the box, the lid was shut and nailed down by the conspirators. They poured melted lead over it and dumped it into the Nile.

As is well-known, the Nile flows from the south to the north of Egypt. It carried the chest containing the body of Osiris to the delta and lodged it firmly in the papyrus swamp upon the Syrian shore at Byblos.

When Osiris did not return from Seth's place, Isis began suspecting foul play. In the meantime, because of indiscretion on the part of some of the co-conspirators of Seth, the word of Osiris' death spread around and reached the ear of Isis overwhelming her with grief.

Isis left the palace and wandered from place to place crying helplessly for her husband and searching for the chest which contained the dead body of Osiris. Her mournful cries made the people of Egypt restless and sad, but no one could tell her about the chest. Ultimately, she arrived close to the delta where a group of children, who had seen a strange box-like object adrift in the Nile waters, told Isis that it had drifted toward Byblos. In the meantime, the chest was cast up into a tree which grew around it.

The tree ultimately attained enormous size and attracted notice of the Syrian king Melcarthus who got it felled to form the main column of his palace. It was an unusual thing in those days, so it became talk of the town and its tale spread far and wide. Isis, on having failed to find the chest in the swamps, invoked her magical and extra-sensory powers to perceive the destiny of the chest containing her husband's body. She had a vision that Osiris's body was hidden within the tree trunk which served as the main column of the King's palace.

On having the vision, Isis rushed to Byblos, the city where the king's palace was situated. She ingratiated herself with the king and the queen of Byblos who were moved at the pathetic tale of the goddess. They gladly permitted Isis to split the tree-trunk column without letting the roof it supported fall to the ground. Isis invoked her magical powers once again, cut the pillar open and extracted the chest.

Osiris (left), and Isis with Horus in her lap.

As soon as she saw the chest, she fell upon it uttering mournful cries. The pathetic scene was too moving for the king Melcarthus and the Queen Astarte to bear. They tried to console Isis, but Isis writhed in agony. She recovered after some time and returned to Egypt with the box.

In Egypt, she took the box to a remote place in the desert and lay the box open. She was once again drowned in grief beyond words when she saw her beloved brother and husband lying lifeless in the chest. She embraced him and wept like a mortal woman.

Isis soon returned to her senses and decided to revive and resurrect Osiris. She assumed the form of a bird; and.........

"She shaded him with her feathers and gave him air with her wings...She cried out for joy and brought her brother to land...She revived the weariness of the Listless One and took his seed into her body, giving him an heir...She suckled the child in secret, the place where he was being unknown."

In the task of reviving Osiris, his wife Isis employed all her magical powers granted to her by her father Thoth. Once Osiris was resurrected, Isis embraced him and took his seed into her womb with the specific purpose to produce Osiris' heir, a son, who would avenge his father's death and reclaim the throne of Egypt from Seth, the killer of his father.

After making Isis pregnant with his seed, Osiris once again lay still and dead. Isis repacked his body in the box and concealed it in a remote and isolated place. In due course of time, Isis gave birth to Osiris' son whom she called Horus. She was overjoyed to look at her son. At this stage her father Thoth visited her and he advised her to keep her own as well as Horus's identity and whereabouts concealed from Seth. Thoth gave her certain magical powers to protect the life of Horus because he knew that Horus would never be far from danger.

Isis, then, left her abode with Horus. Guided and protected by seven scorpions, she brought Horus to a remote island in the papyrus swamp in the Nile delta. Isis had nothing to fall back upon, so she had to leave Horus concealed among the papyrus plants while she was obliged to go to the nearby town to seek food for herself and her child by begging.

One evening, as she returns to the child she finds him sick. She relates her tale in the following manner : "I left him (Horus) alone and wandered alike a beggar woman..... when I returned, expecting to embrace him, I found my beautiful golden Horus, my innocent fatherless child, lying on the ground with water streaming from his eyes and saliva dropping from his lips. His body was limp and his heart was weak, the pulse of his body did not beat."

Isis had no one to call upon for help except the fishermen who lived in the marshes. They came hurrying, and knowing not what to do to alleviate the suffering of Horus, they all wept copiously when they saw Isis lamenting and wailing for the life of her son. Then there came a woman who had a reputation for learning in her city. She approached Isis, looked at Horus and told her that Seth could not approach the province of Chemmis where Isis happened to be living in hiding. The wise woman asked Isis to seek another reason for the suffering of Horus, and she suggested that it might have been a scorpion or a poisonous snake that bit him.

Isis, in the form of large winged bird.

Then Isis examined the breath of the child and found that he had been poisoned. She seized him in her embrace, leaping about with him like fishes that have been put on fire.

Isis raised her hands to the sky and appealed to Re and Thoth to save Horus. Then Thoth came down to her and said, "Do not fear, Divine Isis..... lament not. I have come down from the heaven with the breath of life to cure the child." Then Thoth ordered the poison to be back and exorcized it by the spell of Re. Horus was thus freed from the deadly pcison and restored to life. He grew up to be a healthy young man, skilled in the art of medicine that his mother taught him.

Osiris' Dead Body Hacked

One full-moon night, when Seth was out hunting in the desert, he came upon the chest in which lay the dead body of his brother and enemy Osiris. The chest was hidden there by Isis. Seth recognized it as soon as his eye fell upon it. He opened the box at once and his heart was filled with hatred and rage as he gazed at the dead body of his enemy. He hacked it into 14 pieces and strewed those pieces all over Egypt so that they might not be discovered and assembled by Isis.

Isis soon found that the chest containing the corpse of Osiris was missing. She also heard the tales relating what Seth had done to the corpse of his brother. In this hour of grief and sorrow her sister Nephthys, who was married to Seth, stood by her. Isis, Nephthys and Horus took a papyrus boat and sailed up and down the Nile and wandered throughout Egypt in search of the pieces of Osiris' body. They were successful in their mission. Then they sat down to join the pieces and preserve Osiris' body. Having done that, they buried Osiris properly so that Osiris could pass to the netherworld--the world of the dead.

Horus led his mother Isis and aunt Nephthys to Busiris in the world of the dead. Isis and Nephthys, through exercise of their magical powers, resurrected Osiris. Then Horus restored him full strength and lifted him to the world of gods where Re made him the king of gods and the king of the other world. Horus was also accorded a place amongst the gods.

The Great Quarrel

Once Horus was assured of his rightful place in the assembly of gods, he lay his claim to the kingship of Upper and Lower Egypt which Seth had usurped from Osiris.

The gods kept on discussing the matter for eight decades and failed to arrive at a decision. Finally, Seth and Horus engaged each other in duel in the water having assumed the forms of hippopotamuses. They both submerged in the water. Isis thought that Seth would surely kill Horus, so she fetched a length of rope, tied it to a harpoon and threw it in the water where Seth and Horus had submerged. Then the harpoon pierced the body of Horus, who cried aloud for her mother to withdraw her weapon from him. Isis immediately released him. She cast it again in the water. This time the harpoon pierced the body of Seth who called out in agony : "O Isis, my sister, order your harpoon to release me. I am your brother. I come from the same mother as you, Isis."

Isis' heart was deeply touched and she released Seth. This angered Horus. He emerged from the water, cut off her head and climbed up into the mountain with it. At Re's orders gods chased him in vain, but Seth found him under a tree. He threw him on the ground and gouged his eyes. Later Hathor found Horus lying on the mountain-side.She restored his eyes to him.

Finally, Re decreed in Horus' favour and he was proclaimed king of the Egypt. But Seth was not killed because he was, after all, a stepson of Re and son of Re's wife Nut, the sky-goddess, from Geb, the god of earth. Seth was raised to heaven and made the god of breeze, winds and storm.

Osiris

As for Osiris, he is extolled as Lord of the Universe and essential king. Osiris dwells in the Primeval Mound, which is located in the middle of the world. He has become the master of righteousness. He is treated as the fountain of all living things on earth and in the sky.

Osiris was resurrected but not in his original form as an earthly king. He has become a prototype of liberation of the human soul from the helplessness of death as well as the symbol for liberation of the soul from its psychic hindrances in this life.

Isis was given cow's head by her father Thoth after Horus had severed it from her trunk. When Horus was crowned as the king of Egypt and recognized by gods as the legitimate son and rightful heir to his father Osiris, Isis went to live with her dear brother and husband Osiris in the netherworld. Osiris, Isis and their son Horus lived and ruled happily in their kingdoms thereafter, helping the dead in seeking life in the other world in accordance with the deeds performed by them in their life on earth. ■■

Myths of India-1 : Creation of Human Beings

Indian mythology speaks of three major gods--Brahma,Vishnu and Mahesh--responsible for creation, sustenance and destruction of the universe respectively. The place of Vishnu amongst them is unique. He is held as the prime factor and the primeval force in the creation of the universe. When the formless Brahman assumed form for the first time, he was addressed as Vishnu. He created Prajapati, the prime creator of the cosmos, by dint of volition.

Prior to the creation, the cosmos did not exist. The space was filled with Brahman alone. The Brahman at that stage was formless and therefore nameless. All of a sudden the passive Brahman, the pure consciousness, the eternal existence and bliss par-excellence, developed awareness of being. He wished to be many. Thus began the process of creation of forms and names. Water was created first. Brahman, the primeval male factor known as Nar in Sanskrit language, was responsible for the creation of water. So it was named as Naar. And because the Brahman, on assuming form, took this Naar or water as his Ayana, i.e. abode, he was named Narayana, the water-dweller.

The penetration of Narayana, the primeval male into the naar, the primeval female, produced a huge golden egg, the cosmic egg, leading to the emergence of Brahma, the creator, known as Hiranyagarbha because of his emergence from the golden egg--the golden womb. According to another version of the myth, Narayana or Vishnu was lying on the Shesha Naaga, the celestial serpent, in a state of involution, non-manifestation, non-differentiation or equilibrium--the seed state of the universe and sleep of the Cosmic Soul-when all of a sudden he woke up from his slumber and realized that he was all alone and there was no existence other than himself. He said to himself, "I am one. Let me be many." This idea aroused in Narayana his dormant energy or the rajoguna from which emanated the primeval flow of activity resulting in the emergency of a lotus plant from his navel. The plant flowered and from its flower

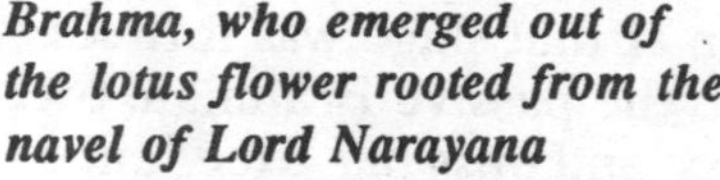

Brahma, who emerged out of the lotus flower rooted from the navel of Lord Narayana

Trimurty, unified form of three Gods : Brahma, Vishnu and Maheshwara.

emerged the Brahma, the primeval agent, through whom Narayana carried out the task of creation of the universe.

After his emergence from the Golden Egg, the Hiranyagarbha or Brahma split the egg into two. From the upper shell, he created the sky and from the lower one he made the earth. The earth was settled upon water. Brahma then created seven sons through mere volition, and he ordered them to create the universe. But his sons, who were in a state of perfect equilibrium, refused to indulge in the task of procreation. This infuriated Brahma, as he was commissioned by Lord Narayana to fulfil his desire for self-manifestation and differentiation in the form of the universe. Brahma's rage produced a child of blue-red hue from his forehead in the middle of his eyebrows. The child at once started weeping, so Brahma named him Rudra, i.e. one who weeps.

Rudra happened to be an angry young god. Brahma called him by 11 names, one of them being Siva, and gave him 11 wives, called Rudraanees. When Brahma called upon Rudra to engage himself in the task of procreation, he went ahead with all seriousness and produced a host of children who were equally angry and destructive by nature. Brahma soon realized the gravity of the situation and cried halt to Rudra. Rudra obeyed and devoted himself to tapasya (penance) as advised by Brahma. It was in this ascetic form that Rudra was called Siva. But as the first creator of the immortal beings, Rudra was considered as the first ancestor of gods.

Then Brahma produced some other children--Narada, Daksha, Vashishtha, Bhrgu, Krti, Pulaha, Pulastya, Angira, Atri and Mareechi respectively from his lap, thumb, breath, skin, hand, navel, ears, mouth, eyes, and mind.

Brahma created numerous other children, including Dharma, Adharma, Kama, Krodha, Lobha and Saraswati (righteousness, evil, lust, anger, greed and the presiding deity of knowledge and speech respectively). Saraswati was an exquisite beauty and she had a pure and chaste mind, yet at her first sight lust was aroused in Brahma's mind. Saraswati pleaded with her father not to indulge in lust and Brahma gave up his body out of disgust and guilt-consciousness. The body Brahma relinquished assumed the form of darkness.

Brahma then took another body, but he continued to be grieved at the universe not expanding fast. He had realized that creatures could not multiply in large numbers without cohabitation between male and female partners. Brahma had a strong urge to create a female, but he feared that if he created a woman he himself might want to have her as it had happened in the case of Saraswati, and then he might have to shed his body once again. He therefore deemed it proper to split his body into two equal halves, and as soon as he thought of it his body was split into two.

One part of Brahma's body was named Manu, the male, and the other part Shatroopa, the female. Manu took Shatroopa as his wife. Essentially it made no difference in the situation. This time Brahma was only half Brahma and Shatroopa was his other half, unlike Saraswati who was an independent goddess and daughter to Brahma. It is from the time of splitting of the body of Brahma and the emergence of Manu and Shatroopa out of it that wife is called Ardhangini (half body) of her husband.

Manu was called Swayambhuva, sui-generis. He mated with Shatroopa and produced five children from her, Priyavrata and Uttanpada—two sons, and Aakooti, Devhooti and Prasooti—three daughters. Aakooti was married with Ruchi Prajapati, Devhooti with sage Kardama, and Prasooti with Daksha Prajapati. The husbands of Manu's daughters were Brahma's sons.

Manu's son Priyavrata was married with the daughter of Vishwakarma Prajapati, another son of Brahma, and Uttanpada with Suruchi and Suneeti, daughters of celestial beings. Uttanpada's son Dhruva became famous for his penance and devotion to god.

Brahman, who took water (naar) as his abode (ayana) was named Narayana.

Thus Manu was the first man and Shatroopa the first woman that appeared on earth and their children were the first human beings that were born on earth from their mother's womb. The entire human race--white or yellow, brown or black, male or female, high caste or low caste, rich or poor, Eastern or Western has Manu and Shatroopa as its first ancestors. According to the myth, man is essentially a part of the creator's being and in no way different from him. Hence the saying: "God has created man in his own image". ■■

Myths of India - 2 : Siva as Chandrashekhara

Siva is one of the three chief gods, the Trimurti--Brahma, Vishnu and Siva--in Indian mythology. Hardly an Indian myth could be conceived of without a role of Siva in it. Siva, along with Brahma, derives his creative attributes from the Vedic figure of Prajapati or the Creator. In Rig Veda, Siva is known as Rudra, and he is invoked as a god of death. At the end of each era (yug) Siva destroys the universe by fire, purifying it by sprinkling it with ashes. Besides, Siva's ascetic nature is most closely tied to his Rudra image.

Siva is both the creator and the destroyer. As creator he is a great lover, represented by the Linga which has become his chief symbol. Siva is said to be permanently ithyphallic, yet perpetually chaste. He is one without any attachments and an all-time ascetic. On the one hand, he destroys Kama Deva, the god of passion and sexual urge, and on the other he longs to marry the mother goddess Parvati. These are the two socalled opposing strands of Siva's nature. The Siva of Brahmin philosophy is predominantly ascetic; the Siva of Tantric cult is predominantly sexual. This ambivalence of his character is best represented in a patent myth about Siva in which he is born as a man named Chandrashekhara.

Beaten at Dice

Siva once played the game of dice with his consort Parvati and was badly beaten by her at the game. Siva then went naked and alone into the woods. When he was gone, Parvati was tortured by longing and thought only of Siva. She was tormented by the thought that she had won Siva through great tapas but had cheated him at dice. She then took the form of a voluptuously beautiful woman. When Siva saw her, he tried to grab her by hand, for he was aroused from his meditation and was full of desire, but Parvati vanished. Then Siva wandered about in delusion, full of lust and longing. He met the mountain woman again and asked her who she was. She said, "I seek a husband who knows every thing, is independent, and is free from emotions." Siva said, "I am the husband you seek." But she smiled and said, "You are quite different from the man I seek.

You have abandoned in the forest the woman who had won you with her tapas."

Siva wanted her to be his wife, but she refused and mocked at him telling him that he was rich in tapas, a great yogi and one who was without passion and had even burnt down the god of lust--Kama Deva. Siva once again tried to take her by force, but she escaped this time also.

Parvati left Siva to perform tapas in order to obtain a golden skin for her body, and Siva was tormented by lust for her and sought her in vain. One day, deluded by Kama, Siva saw the beautiful Savitri who resembled Parvati, and mistaking her for Parvati, he begged her to make love with him. He tried to take her by force, but Savitri was a chaste goddess. She scolded him saying, "You should apologise to your wife instead of trying to take another man's wife. Since you have tried to seduce me, behaving like a human being, you will have to make love to a mortal woman."

Savitri's curse opened Siva's eyes. He felt ashamed and returned to his abode on the Meru mountain. It was because of Savitri's curse that he had to take birth as Chandrashekhara, a human being, and he had to make love with a mortal woman Tarawati.

Trayambaka or Chandrashekhara

Once upon a time a king, who had no son, worshipped and propitiated Siva who gave him a fruit which was to be divided into three equal parts, one to be given to each of the king's three queens. The king did likewise and his wives consumed the fruit. The king then made love to each one of them at the appropriate season of the year, and all of them became pregnant. Each one of them delivered, after nine months, a third of a child and miraculously all the parts united at their own and became one child. The king and the queens were highly delighted to see the child who was named Trayambaka because he was born of three mothers. He was also named Chandrashekhara because he had Moon as his diadem just as Siva has had.

In due course of time, Chandrashekhara attained manhood. His parents retired to forest to do tapas, and Chandrashekhara was given charge of the kingdom as the new king. He married Tarawati, an incarnation of Parvati.

One day, when Tarawati was bathing in the river, she was seen by a sage named Kapota, who was overcome by lust for her. He thought she must be a goddess or a demon who had assumed human form in order to enjoy pleasures of the flesh, and he told her accordingly. He asked her, "Which one of the two you are--Parvati or Sachi (wife of Indra)?" Tarawati replied, "I am neither. I am a mortal woman, wife of king Chandrashekhara." Kapota, blinded by lust for Tarawati, expressed his desire before her. He promised to reward her with two sons, strong and handsome.

Tarawati was in a fix. On one side there was a sage asking for love and promising her two sons, and on the other she was afraid of the consequences on two counts. These counts were: first, she was a married woman, and the second, it would have been a sin to make love with a sage and thus become instrumental in the undoing of his tapasya. She, therefore, warned the sage that he should desist from such a course as it would do harm to his penance. But the sage was determined to make love to her irrespective of the consequences. He said, "You must save me from Kama Deva, or he will burn me and then I will burn you with a curse."

Tarawati was frightened, but she took courage and left the place promising to return in a little while. Tarawati did not want to be disloyal to her husband. She sent her sister Chitrangada dresseed and disguised as Tarawati to the sage. The sage was deluded by lust. He made love to Chitrangada and taking her as Tarawati promised to deliver her of the sin of adultery by virtue of his penance. Chitrangada gave birth to two sons. The sons were raised by the sage, and Chitrangada stayed with him.

After some time Tarawati returned to the river and, as she was bathing in its waters, the sage Kapota again saw her. It was then that he became aware of the fraud played upon him by the queen. He was enraged and he cursed Tarawati, "Since you humiliated me thinking yourself to be so virtuous and inviolate and too good to desire me, Siva shall visit you and make love to you by force in his terrifying garments and you shall bear him a pair of monkey-faced sons then and there."

Tarawati was by heart a virtuous wife. She said to the sage, "I swear by my true vows to my husband Chandrashekhara that I will never allow any one but him to make love to me even in a dream. I swear this by the vows that my father made to Parvati when he obtained me for his daughter."

The sage listened to the queen in rapt attention and he immediately went into samadhi. In his samadhi he realized the truth that Tarawati was none else but goddess Parvati and Chandrashekhara was lord Siva. He opened his eyes, begged pardon of the queen and left the place along with Chitrangada and her two sons. He honoured Chitrangada and took her as his lawful wife.

Siva Visits Tarawati

Tarawati's conscience was clear as she had nothing to hide. She took her husband Chandrashekhara into confidence about Kapota's lustful advances towards her. She also told him about the curse the sage Kapota had hurled at her. Chandrashekhara took extra care for the security of his wife. he made a high terrace on the top of his palace in order to make her unapproachable by anyone. Deluded by Maya, Chandrashekhara failed to realize that he himself was Siva and there was nothing that could check a powerful god like Siva from reaching the palace terrace.

One day Tarawati stood on the terrace thinking of her husband and offering her prayers to Lord Siva and his celestial consort Parvati. All of a sudden she was filled with the idea that Siva and Chandrashekhara are one and the same. She could not distinguish between the two. While Tarawati stood pondering on the identities of Siva and her husband, Lord Siva arrived there accompanied by Parvati. Siva told Parvati that Tarawati was her mortal incarnation. He asked her to enter the body of Tarawati in her subtle form as he wanted to make love with Tarawati and produce two sons from her.

Parvati immediately complied with the wishes of her husband and Siva approached Tarawati to make love to her in the form of a shabbily dressed kapalika wearing a foul-smelling garland of skulls. Tarawati was already possessed by the spirit of Parvati. She did not resist the advances of the kapalika. She received him with great joy and later gave birth to his two sons with monkey faces.

After making love to Tarawati and producing two sons from her, Siva left the place with Parvati. It was then that Tarawati realized what had happened to her. When she found that she had given birth to two sons from the kapalika, she was filled with a sense of mortal guilt. Seeing her in such a morbid state of mind, Siva reappeared before her and said to her, "You should not entertain any sort of guilt in your heart for having made love to me. I am Siva. You had vowed before kapota, the sage, that you would never desire any man other than Chandrashekhara. Your vow has not been vio-

Siva, dancing along with Vaitala, Bhairava and other attendents (ganas).

lated because I am Siva and I am also Chandrashekhara. Do not grieve." But after Siva had left, she was again deluded and she wept in grief and anger over what had happened to her.

On Chandrashekhara's return to the palace, Tarawati related the entire episode to him. Chandrashekhara wondered what all this meant. He was sure that Siva loved his celestial consort and he could not make love to any woman other than Parvati. He thought that the curse hurled upon his wife by the sage Kapota was very powerful. He thought that probably some demon was sent disguised as Siva to materialise the curse and it was this demon who had defiled his wife and sired two demon-like children form her.

The king was lost in thoughts like this when goddess Saraswati, the celestial daughter of Brahma, arrived there and assured the king that Siva himself had visited his wife, made love to her and produced the two children. Chandrashekhara was now relaxed and he raised the two sons as his own. Then he was visited by Narada who explained to him how Siva was born as Chandrashekhara and Parvati as Tarawati because of Savitri's curse. Narada made both of them realize who they were, and thus they arrived at perfect understanding with each other.

But they could not overcome their natural propensities as mortal human beings. As time went by, Chandrashekhara began to fear that the two monkey-faced sons could harm their three natural sons, so he began to show greater favour to his natural sons.

Siva's sons had a feeling of mortification at the king's discrimination against them. So they went away and performed tapas which induced Siva to visit them. He bestowed immortality upon them and made them captains of his devotees. They are known till this day as Vaitala and Bhairava. ■■

Myths of India - 3 : Vedvati's Vow

Lord Vishnu lay passively upon Sheshnaag in the primeval waters known as Ksheer Sagar, the sea of milk. Once he developed an urge to become many and he began to multiply. Lord Vishnu caused a lotus plant to emerge from his navel and out of the lotus flower emerged Brahma, the Prajapati or the creator of the universe.

Brahma, in turn, created marine life. But those creatures had nothing to live upon, so they went to Brahma and requested him to provide them with food. Brahma, after making necessary arrangements, asked his children to protect the waters. At this, some of the water-creatures said they would worship the water, while others promised the Prajapati to defend the water. Prajapati Brahma, thereupon, divided the water-creatures into two communities. Those who opted to worship the water were called by him Yaksha, and those who promised to defend the water were named Rakshasa.

The Yakshas were very close to the heart of Lord Vishnu, and also worshipped Lord Siva in his ascetic form. The Rakshasas, on the other hand, were jealous of Lord Vishnu and they worshipped Lord Siva in his Rudra--angry--form. Soon the Rakshasas, who were assigned the task of raksha or protection of god's creation, became unruly and they began to torment other creatures, particularly the Yakshas.

Among the Yakshas there was a Pulastya, a Brahmin, who was a great and celebrated sage of his times. Pulastya's son Vishrava was also a known sage. He was married to the daughter of another sage Bhardwaj. From her he had a son Vaishravan who later became famous as Kuber, the treasurer of the Yakshas. Brahma granted Kuber a status equal to Indra and Varun and Yama equal to Lokpal, guardian of the cosmic order.

Kuber's father Vishrava assigned the kingdom of Lanka to him. Lanka was built by Vishwakarma, the divine builder for the Rakshasas. The Rakshasas had fled Lanka frightened by Vishnu, but after

Kuber established his rule over the island, the Rakshasas returned there with the permission of Kuber and accepted him as their king. But at heart the Rakshasas wanted a Rakshasa as their ruler. One of their chieftains named Sumali, eager to reestablish Rakshasa hegemony over Lanka, planned meticulously to overthrow Kuber.

Sumali asked his young and beautiful daughter Kaikasi to take the sage Vishrava as husband so as to have children from him as strong and as wealthy as Kuber. Kaikasi, obedient to her father, arrived at the ashrama of the sage in the evening when the sage was preparing for the evening yajna. She told him that she was sent to him by her father. The sage went into samadhi and was disgusted to discover the cause of her visit. He tried to persuade Kaikasi to wait till an opportune moment to have him as her husband and make love to her because love-making in the evening was destined to produce terribly violent and demonic beings. But Kaikasi was hell-bent upon having the sage right then and there. The sage fulfilled her desire and when she prayed to him falling at his feet to bless the children she had conceived from him, Vishrava said, "O beautiful damsel, of others I cannot say a thing, but I bless your youngest one who will follow the traditions of his father."

Afterwards Kaikasi gave birth to four children. The eldest was born with ten heads, twenty arms and large teeth protruding from the extremities of his mouth. He was named Dashagreeva, later called by Siva as Ravana. The second son, named Kumbhakarna,was born with an immense body. The third child was a daughter named Shoorpanakha. The fourth child was a son, Vibheeshana. At the birth of Vibheeshana gods expressed their joy by showering flowers upon him and presenting a musical orchestra from heaven.

Kuber Defeated

Ravana became jealous of Kuber. He wanted the kingdom of Lanka returned to the Rakshasas. Ravana was a Rakshasa himself. He did not inherit the Yaksha traits of his father; on the contrary he inherited the Rakshasa traits of his mother's side. He sent a message to his elder brother Kuber demanding the reigns of Lanka for himself. Kuber did not object. He renounced the kingdom and went to Kailas where he established his second kingdom. Ravana was thus crowned the Rakshasa king of Lanka. Ravana had acquired wealth and power both. He became haughty and wanted to capture Kuber's second kingdom too. Kuber was defeated by Ravana in a grim battle and Ravana returned to Lanka with Kuber's Pushpak Viman--

aeroplane as light as a flower--as his trophy. The Pushpak provided him with easy accessibility to any corner of the universe.

In search of further conquests, one day Ravana arrived at the Sharvan--the famous reed jungle--the birth place of the great yogi Kartikeya, Siva's son. There the Pushpak lost its capacity to fly further due to the magnetic pull of the hill below. This angered Ravana. He got down and went into the camp of Lord Siva to discover as to who had dared to stop his aeroplane from flying further. He was met with Nandishwar, the celestial bull Siva rode. Nandishwar warned Ravana to dare not enter the Siva camp. Ravana did not listen to him. He went ahead and attempted to uproot and throw aside the Mount Meru, the great magnetic force which had prevented Pushpak from flying across it. Lord Siva was, at that time, engaged in celestial play with his divine consort Parvati. As Ravana tried to lift the mount in his arms, the mount shook terribly frightening goddess Parvati and Siva's attendants. Siva was not at all disturbed. He simply pressed the mount with the toe of his right leg.

The mount settled down once again and Ravana's arms buried under it. Ravana cried out with pain. Seeing their king in a miserable plight, the senior ministers of Ravana's court in attendance advised him to recite hymns in praise of Lord Siva in order to please him. Ravana had no other alternative before him. He began praying to Lord Rudra who, instantly pleased with him, released his arms from under the mountain and offered to bless him with whatever was wanted by him. Ravana wanted Siva to bless him with long life and one of his invincible weapons. Siva blessed him with both. He gave him his powerful Chandrahasa sword.

Confrontation with Vedvati

Having won Siva's pleasure, Ravana wandered in the Himalayan regions. There he came across a young ascetic damsel given to penance and as bright as a goddess. As he saw the girl, Ravana's heart was filled with lust. He roared with laughter and mocked at her penance at that tender and young age.

The girl gave Ravana respect due to a stranger. She introduced herself as the daughter of the realized sage Kushadhwaja, the son of god Brihaspati, who was as brilliant as his father. The girl told Ravana that she was born with memory of Veda texts. It was for this reason that she was named Vedavati.

Vedvati said further, "When I grew up, gods, Gandharvas,

Rakshasas, Yakshas and Nagas came to my father and sought my hand. But my father refused every one of them, because he wanted Lord Vishnu, the king of gods and master of all the three spheres, as his son-in-law. When Shambhu, one of the demon kings who considered himself the mightiest of all the gods and humans, came to know of my father's resolve, he killed him while he was asleep in the night. My mother was severely grieved at my father's death and she mounted on the funeral pyre with her husband's dead body held fast to her chest and thus ended her life.

"Since then I am pledged to redeem my father's will toward Lord Narayana, and I adore him in my heart. I am doing penance with a vow to wed Vishnu. Narayana is my husband. No other person could aspire to have me as his wife. I have identified you. You are the grandson of the renowned sage Pulastya. I am aware of whatever exists in the three spheres of this universe through my penance--tapas."

Ravana then alighted from the Pushpak Viman and, stung by the arrows of Kama Deva, asked Vedvati to accept him as her husband. He spoke of Vishnu in derogatory terms. Vedvati asked him to shut up. Her defence of Vishnu enraged the haughty Rakshasa who stepped forward and held Vedvati by hair.

Vedvati was enraged too. She cut off her hair by a single movement of her hand. Then she lit an immense fire and said, "O mean rakshasa, you have insulted me. I shall keep this body no more. I shall enter this fire that I have lit by force of my penance before your eyes. You are a great sinner. I shall take birth again to have you slayed. I do not want to hurl a curse upon you as it may dampen my tapas. If I have lived a righteous life, let me be reborn without being conceived by a mother, and let me have an enlightened sage as my father."

Having spoken thus, Vedvati entered the fire she had lit. Gods from heaven showered flowers upon her funeral pyre.

Rebirth as Sita

As desired by her, Vedvati had her rebirth without being conceived and delivered by a human mother. She was conceived by a lotus and appeared from its flower as a beautiful and bright girl.

Ravana picked the girl from the lotus flower and took her home. There he showed her to his minister who was an expert in the

Ravana, encirled by the vow of Vedvati.

study of characteristics of children. He examined the girl thoroughly and told Ravana that if the girl remained in his palace she would bring him ruin and death.

On hearing this Ravana threw the girl into the sea from where she was deposited at the shore by the sea waves and accepted by the mother earth. The mother earth, in turn, deposited her in the central pavilion of the oblations-square (yajna mandapa) of Janaka, the king of Mithila.

The girl surfaced as king Janaka's plough furrowed the pavilion on the occasion of ceremonial tilling by the king. As she had appeared out of the furrow, she was named Sita. Sita was no other than Vedvati reincarnate. Before entering the fire, Vedvati had taken two vows--to wed Lord Vishnu and to cause slaying of Ravana. She fulfilled both the vows in her reincarnation as Sita.

After her appearance out of the furrow, Sita was well looked after and taken care of in the household of king Janaka, and the king loved his daughter immensely. But his decision to give Sita to one who succeeded in mounting a cord on the mighty bow of Lord

Siva could have brought her once again very close to the clutches of Ravana had he chosen to vie for Sita's hand and bend Siva's bow to put a cord upon it. Thankfully, Ravana did not participate in the contest.

Ultimately, Vedvati, reincarnated as Sita, got an opportunity to fulfil her second vow--to cause Ravana's death. Instead of avoiding Sita, Ravana kidnapped her like a thief from Panchvati and thus invited ruin upon his people and himself. Vedvati was thoroughly avenged. To this day, Ravana is hated as a demon and Vedvati's curse is still upon him. Ravana is slayed and thrown to flames every year in every nook and corner of India. No other crime in human history has received such wider condemnation as Ravana's show of lust toward Sita, and no other curse prevails and persists with such intensity from year to year as Vedvati's upon Ravana which has persisted and prevailed for nearly 5000 years at a stretch. ■■

Greek Mythology - 1 : Zeus

Greek civilization is rooted in ancient past. It is very rich as regards myths. The myths of Greece have earned universal popularity. Zeus is the first Greek god who destroyed the gods existing before him and established a new divine order which is properly known as the Greek Divinity.

Greeks believed that originally there was emptiness. It was out of this emptiness that three immortal beings emerged: Gaea, the mother earth; Tartarus, the lord of the netherworld; and Eros, the god of love whose inspiration was behind all creation immortal and mortal.

Gaea, at her own without any male partner, produced the male god Uranus, the god of sky, and took her as husband. Besides Uranus, Gaea gave birth to Ourea, the mountains, and Pontus, the seas.

From her union with Uranus the mother-goddess Gaea gave birth to her six children--three Giants, each with 50 heads and hundred hands, and three Cyclopes, each with one eye in the forehead. The Cyclopes were master craftsmen who built the palaces for gods on Mount Olympus. These six children of Uranus and Gaea were immortal. Uranus was afraid as well as jealous of his children. He feared they would snatch from his hands his power over earth. So at the time of each child's birth, Uranus hurled him into the being of mother Earth--Gaea. Each child fell for nine days and nine nights and reached the netherworld ruled by Lord Tartarus on the tenth day. He did not allow them to see the sunlight.

Mother goddess Gaea was displeased and outraged at this brutal action of her husband Uranus. She wanted her children back and waited for the appropriate moment to take her revenge upon Uranus. The couple produced 13 other immortal children known as Titans. Cronus, the youngest of the Titans, was a courageous god and brute like his father Uranus. Of all the children, he alone came forward to help his mother Gaea in facing Uranus. Gaea gave a flint sickle to Cronus for use as a weapon in his fight against his father. Cronus was not unduly concerned about the manner in which Uranus imprisoned the six immortal children of Gaea in the territory of Tartarus. He joined hands with Gaea to kill Uranus as he saw in it an opportunity to assume the kingship of gods in place of his father.

One day, at the dead of night, Uranus lay asleep by the seashore. At that time Cronus, who was hiding nearby behind a bush, rushed forward and severed the male organs of his father with a flint sickle. He threw the parts into the sea and told his father that his reign was over and that he had taken over the reigns of the universe into his hands. Cronus advised Uranus to submit to him. Uranus was helpless. Cronus, thus, became god of the sky, but he refused to obey his mother when she asked him to bring the Giants and the Cyclopes back to earth from the netherworld. It would be found interesting to note that the private parts of Uranus thrown in the sea by Cronus gave birth to Aphrodite, the goddess of beauty, love and sexual infatuation, also called Venus by the Romans.

Cronus imitates Uranus

Cronus, then, married his sister Rhea. He loved Rhea, but he did not want to have any children for the simple reason that his mother Gaea, who was also the goddess of prophecy and angry with Cronus at his refusal to free his brothers from the netherworld, had forecast that Cronus would one day be deprived of his throne by one of his sons in the manner he himself had behaved toward his father.

In due course of time, Rhea gave birth to a daughter Hestia and presented the child to Cronus. Prompted by the prophecy, Cronus decided to do away with the child and gulped her instantly without giving a thought to the fact that the child was a girl. He did not want to take chances.

One by one four more children--Demeter, Hera, Hades and Posidon--were born to Rhea from Cronus and each time Cronus swallowed the child. Rhea was quite upset and grieved. She approached her mother Gaea and asked for her help in the matter. Gaea told Rhea that she was carrying a son in her womb and that the boy was destined to do away with the injustice perpetrated upon her by Cronus. Gaea advised Rhea to hide in a cave on the slopes of Mount Dicte at Crete and to deliver the child in the cave. Gaea promised Rhea that after her return to Cronus, she would see that nymphs took care of her son and fed him on goat milk.

Nymphs, protecting Zeus under the supervision of Gaea (sitting); and Zeas drinking goat milk.

Rhea acted upon her mother's advice. Then on her return to Cronus, she wrapped a rock of her infant son's size in a cloth and handed it over to Cronus telling him that it was his son borne by her. Cronus was almost mad to hear Rhea. He took the rock into his hands, embraced it and swallowed it in one gulp. He was glad assuming that he had once again fooled the destiny.

Cronus never knew that one of his sons had escaped from his clutches and was being brought up by the nymphs in Crete. The child was named Zeus by his mother. When he became a mature god, Rhea called him to her palace and entered into a conspiracy with him to bring her children back from the netherworld and deprive Cronus of his reign as sky-god. One day Cronus asked Rhea to serve him a drink. Rhea offered him one, and on Cronus' asking for more, the second drink was offered by Zeus. After taking the drink Cronus had strange sensation in his stomach and he began vomiting. The first object to emerge from his stomach was a rock and then his five grown up children followed one by one.

It was at this point that Rhea introduced Zeus to Cronus as his son and told him that he was not able to fool the destiny and that a son of his was there to replace him as ruler of the gods. Cronus challenged Zeus to have a fight with him.

Rhea, offering Cronus a rock wrapped around with her infant son's cloths.

Zeus was in a fix. The gods (Zeus and his brothers and sisters) and the Titans (Cronus and his brothers and sisters) were evenly matched in strength. Zeus, therefore, could not hope to win the war over the years. To resolve this problem, Gaea advised her grandchild Zeus to bring his six uncles back from the netherworld and win the fight against his father with their help.

Zeus followed her advice, went to the land of Tartarus, rescued his uncles and brought them back to earth. The legendary fight between the gods and the Titans started. It was a terrible war. It shook mountains and caused upheavals across the earth and the sea. Finally, the Titans were hurled into the Tartarus' territory and chained for ever to remain there in the dark underworld. Two of the Giants, sons of Gaea, volunteered to guard the Titans in the Tartarus while the third Giant Atlas was employed to hold the sky high on his shoulders.

Then Zeus decided to clearly earmark the kingdoms of his own and his two brothers--Poseidon and Hades. They drew lots. Zeus got the sky, Poseidon and sea and Hades the netherworld. Zeus had three sisters--Hera, Hestia and Demeter. He married Hera and loved Demeter, the goddess of foodgrains. Hestia became the guardian of homes and morals. She remained a virgin.

Zeus The Lover

In Greek mythology, Zeus has been depicted as the Father God and the dominant male-god who, though married to his sister Hera, took a number of women as his beloved including his other sister Demeter. Zeus sired a galaxy of gods like Apollo, Artemis, Athena, Persephone, Dionysus, and mortals like Heracles, Helen and Perseus.

One of the greatest loves of Zeus was Leto, a goddess. Zeus became infatuated with her and made her pregnant. When Hera, wife of Zeus, came to know of the affair, she decided to punish Leto. Hera pursued her for many months driving her from one country to another and never allowing her to rest. But at last some of the gods were so moved by Leto's sufferings that they decided to help her find a land where she could remain in peace. The only spot they could think of was a small island afterwards called Delos which, curiously enough, had been floating about for many years in the Aegean sea. Here Leto got settled and here her children, Apollo and his twin sister Artemis, were born. Zeus was so fond of the island that he fastened it to other islands and made it stationary as it is today.

Zeus had developed great affection and love for Semele, daughter of a king of Thebes. Semele had already conceived from Zeus when Hera, wife of Zeus, got jealous of her and decided to destroy her. Hera visited her one day disguised as Semele's aged nurse. Eager to confide her happy secret to friendly ears, Semele poured forth the story of her good fortune in having as her lover no less a person than Zeus, the king of gods himself. Hera, as her old nurse, advised Semele to test the identity of her lover. She said to Semele, "I should advise you to ascertain his identity by asking him to appear to you some day in his royal garb, wearing the divine armour and equipped with his powerful thunderbolt." The idea pleased Semele and on the occasion of Zeus' next visit, Semele said to him: "Grant me a favour, Zeus, even though you know not what it is to be." Zeus assented. No sooner, however, had Semele started to express her wish that Zeus realized his mistake. He tried to dissuade her from putting her desire into words, but it was too late. She had already conveyed the meaning of her request.

Zeus knew that Semele, a mortal woman, could not withstand the heat of his thunderbolt, and would surely perish if exposed to it, but he dared not break a god's word. Accordingly, he appeared to the maiden in all his awful splendour but before the flames reduced Semele to ashes, Zeus rescued her unborn baby and brought him up. He named him Dionysus. Romans call him Bacchus. He is worshipped as the god of vegetation and alcoholic drinks.

Zeus once saw a maiden Europa playing in the fields with her companions. So great was his admiration for her beauty that he was determined to carry the girl away. In order to avoid arousing suspicion in her about his plan, he changed himself into a white bull and by various devices tempted the girl to mount upon his back. He, then, ran swiftly away, finally reaching a land which in honour of the maiden he named Europa. Till this day, this place is known as the continent of Europe.

From another beloved woman Maia, Zeus sired Hermes (Mercury) who became protector of heralds and travellers. Once Zeus felt a severe pain in his head for which he was unable to account. Soon, however, the goddess Athena (Minerva) sprang forth, radiant in beauty and wearing the full armour of a warrior. Athena founded the city of Athens.

Zeus had very close love-relation with Alcmene, a distinguished woman and wife of Amphitryon. Zeus had a son, Heracles, from Alcmene. He wanted to make him immortal, but he dared not displace Hera, his wife, who hated his other women and his children from them. When Heracles was only eight months old, Hera, wishing to kill him, sent two huge snakes into his nursery. As the snakes approached his bed, Heracles grabbed a snake in each of his hands and strangled both serpents. Heracles had to pass through severe tests of his skill and strength before he was made immortal and assigned a place at Mount Olympus amongst gods.

Creator of Human Beings

Zeus, the father and the king of immortal gods, was also the creator of human beings. He is said to have created five generations of human beings corresponding to five ages or stages of human civilization-Race of Gold, Race of Silver, Race of Bronze, Race of Heroes and the Race of Iron. The race of gold lived in the golden age marked by highest virtues and human values acquired by human beings in the natural course. The race of gold was self-disciplined; it needed neither law nor judicial courts and police. Peace reigned on earth. The human life was treated as the highest value and human beings were free from greed, hatred, slavery and grief of any kind. It

Zeus, creator of five Races and human civilizations on this earth.

was an age of divine grace and opulence as rivers of milk and nectar flowed on earth and trees dripped honey at their own. Pastures were green and cattle and sheep were in abundance. Human beings were not acquisitive by nature and they had no need to build defences, armies and weapons. They were free from disease and they died peacefully as if death were a state of gentle and eternal slumber.

When this golden age or the Satyuga was over, Zeus created the silver race as the second generation of human beings. In this second age, man had lost his innocence and he had become quarrelsome. This angered Zeus and in order to punish the silver race he brought an end to the eternal spring and ordered the year to be divided into four seasons. It was in this age that man had to build houses and plough fields with the help of oxen to grow food. The life span of human beings was made short and after death their souls were consigned to the netherworld. It was in this age that man experienced want, misery, suffering and conflict for the first time.

The third generation produced by Zeus is known as the bronze race. With the advent of this race an era of war, violence, destruction and cruelty began on earth and the human civilization declined further.

Then Zeus produced a superior race, the race of heroes, which fought for higher causes and was more virtuous and noble-hearted than the silver and bronze races. Zeus blessed the heroes with an eternal life of peace and bliss.

According to the myth, Zeus finally produces the iron race bringing upon earth the dark age with it--an age full of eternal grief and sorrow, greed and avarice, struggle and strife, disease and death, crime and violence, cruelty and injustice. According to the myth, the iron race or the race of Kali as predicted in the Indian mythology, was predicted to be marked by selfishness and acquisitiveness. This race was destined to suffer from dissatisfaction with whatever the mother earth produced for it, and in its endeavour to acquire more and more wealth it was bound to rip open the heart of the mother earth and plunder the wealth hidden underneath, to invade the heavens and pollute and plunder other planets. The iron race was destined to be destroyed in internecine wars. In this age, parents and their children were predicted to become devoid of filial love and respect because of acute differences between them. Children in this age were to show no concern for their aged parents and elders, and the virtuous were to find no place in the order of the day.

We, the present inhabitants of the earth, belong to the iron race or the generation of the age of Kali. The part of the myth which applies to our age holds true. According to the myth, Zeus might one day discover us to be the most unworthy of being his children and undeserving to inherit earth, and so destroy us. Perhaps this time he may not be required to take the trouble of destroying the human race as we, his children, are foolish enough to destroy ourselves. The dark cloud of ego and love of materialism has completely shrouded our innate divine spark and intelligence, and we are so wholeheartedly given to the production of means of mass annihilation of life on earth and other planets that destruction of the present human generation is almost certain. Zeus has, perhaps, chosen to act through us this time. May he exercise his discretion and, instead of making the human race extinct from the face of earth, change our hearts and minds and make us conform to the laws of nature and obey his command. ■■

Greek Mythology - 2 : Persephone

Demeter, daughter of Cronus, the deposed sky god, and sister of Zeus, the new ruler of sky, was the goddess of the green things of earth, the plants, the grass, and the trees, and particularly the produce of fields. She caused the seasons to operate at the proper time. She ardently loved creatures of the earth and the earth that fed them. She was in turn greatly loved by the mortals. In Greece, every farmer's wife would always serve an extra plate on the dining table fervently hoping that Demeter would knock at their door and join the family at evening meals. Demeter was very kind to farmers. She looked after their crops and saw that they flourished and yielded abundantly at the harvest time. It was Demeter who taught men to plough the fields and sow them with seeds in order to reap harvests. She also taught them the art and science of animal husbandry. Whenever there was a festival or festivity in the house of a farmer, the altar of Demeter was profusely offered gifts of fruit, grain and freshly baked loaves set aside for her by the farmers' wives. Gods would always tease her that she was a great eater and particularly eat her meals in the humble homes of mortals than in the palaces of gods at Mount Olympus.

Demeter had a lovely and wonderful daughter Persephone from her brother and lover Zeus. Persephone was the apple of her eyes. She loved sunshine, flowers and pleasure. Persephone would always fill the lives of all those who loved her and who were known to her with pleasure. She used to roam about the wild flower fields in Sicily with a basket in her hand to fill it with the flowers. On such jaunts, she was accompanied by her step-sisters Artemis and Athena.

Once, on a sunny day, Persephone happened to be picking flowers with her companions in a field. She wandered about quite carefree and happy as some blossom, unusually perfect in form or colouring, caught her fancy. Just about that time Hades, lord of the netherworld and brother of Zeus, chanced to pass through that way. He was on a visit to the earth in order to find out if giant Typhoon, who lay on his back under Mount Aetna vomiting fire, had created any cracks in the earth through which the light of sun could reach the netherworld terrifying the souls living there under the care of Hades.

It was there that Hades saw Persephone Her exotic and divine beauty aroused love in his dreary heart as Eros, at the orders of her mother Aphrodite who wanted Hades to fall in love, had aimed one of his arrows at his heart. Hades did not know how to secure the hand of Persephone. So he went to his brother Zeus and sought his permission to marry his daughter. Zeus knew that her mother Demeter would never agree to such a marriage because she loved earth and her creatures and life was not possible on earth in absence of Persephone who caused seeds to sprout and plants to grow and flower through her laughter. Demeter knew that Persephone loved sunshine and she could not live happily in the dark netherworld where sun never ventured to show. So Zeus proposed to Hades that if he dared to seize Perspehone, he would assist him in the task secretly. Hades accepted the proposal and went back to his kingdom and waited for an appropriate opportunity to seize Persephone.

One day, when Persephone was gathering flowers in the meadow, her eye fell upon a narcissus flower at some distance. It was a beautiful flower and Persephone was very fond of it. She left her companions behind and ran over the meadow to gather the flower she was infatuated with. Persephone had no idea that the flower was created at that time by her father Zeus through his divine and magical powers as a part of the conspiracy he had entered into with his brother Hades, the lord of wealth, in order to keep him humoured so that he continued to bless the mankind with wealth. Hades is also known as Pluto (derived from Latin Pluton, pronounced in Greek as `Plouton', which means wealth).

As Persephone reached the spot where the narcissus flower was blooming and picked the flower, she saw to her amazement and horror that the ground was opening, and before she could call for help the chasm widened. In no time coal-black steeds of gigantic size sprang forth and a chariot appeared in which Hades, her uncle and god of the underworld stood smiling at her. In an instant Persephone was seized in the god's strong arms. Hades lifted her off the ground, placed her beside him in his chariot and drove off at breakneck speed before Athena and Artemis could realize that Hades had abducted Persephone.

Persephone helplessly cried. She called for her mother and

Hades, abducting Persephone.

father but they were far away and her screams did not reach their ears. Still, she kept on calling her mother. Only Sun, high above in the sky, witnessed the crime. When Athena and Artemis reached the spot, the chasm had already closed and Persephone had disappeared leaving behind her basket full of exotic flowers.

Persephone's cries continued to echo from high mountains and issue forth from the depths of sea, and they reached the ears of Demeter, her mother. Demeter was mad to hear her daughter's cries and she desperately ran here and there in search of Persephone. For nine days and nine nights, she searched unwearingly but could find no trace of her.

Demeter then went to Sicily from where Persephone had disappeared and when Sicilians failed to tell her anything about her daughter, she decided to punish them. She broke their ploughs, killed their oxen and ordered the earth to retain the seeds and prevent them from sprouting. Sicily's fields were left devastated and barren by the angry goddess. Demeter was completely out of joint at the loss of her daughter and she poured out her wrath upon the whole earth causing ruin to all life. There was acute drought all around and not a single seed sprouted, not a single blade of grass remained green on earth.

Finally Demeter approached Lord Helios (Sun) and asked him if he had any idea of her daughter's whereabouts. She told him that from the desperate cries of Persephone she had concluded that she was taken away by someone forcibly. She beseeched of sun god to tell her the truth. Helios narrated the entire episode to her and added that it was Zeus himself who had given his daughter to his brother Hades, lord of the netherworld, to be his wife and queen of the dead and goddess of wealth. Sun informed Demeter that Hades had forcibly abducted her daughter who kept crying until earth closed upon them. Sun advised Demeter to take heart as there was nothing to grieve about--after all Hades was her brother and lord of a mighty kingdom. He counselled her to give up her anger and recover from her grief.

Demeter Strikes Work

On hearing from Lord Helios that it was Zeus who permitted and helped Hades in the abduction of Persephone by him, Demeter was enraged. Her heart was seething with grief at her daughter's abduction to the world of the dead. In order to avenge the wrong done to her by Zeus, Demeter finally decided to strike work and let all the mortals die of starvation so that there would remain no one to offer sacrifices to gods.

As soon as Zeus came to know of Demeter's intention, he sent his messenger to ask Demeter to return to Mount Olympus and present herself before the king of gods. Demeter refused to comply with the orders of Zeus. Then Zeus sent other gods one after the other to persuade Demeter to appear before him. Demeter refused all but the last one of them whom she asked to convey her message to Zeus--that she was willing to see Zeus but she would not let a single seed sprout unless she had seen the face of her daughter.

Demeter appeared before Zeus and requested him in a humble tone to restore their daughter to her, to sunshine, to meadows rich in flowers and to life. She told him that Persephone always loved life so she should not have been condemned to live in the world of the dead. She also registered her protest at the manner Hades had abducted her with the intention of marrying her. Demeter asked Zeus as to how he could permit Hades to marry Persephone when he had abducted her against her will. She pleaded for the return of Persephone to earth.

Zeus tried to persuade Demeter to let Hades have her daughter as his wife and forgive him for his having abducted Persephone keeping in view the fact that Hades loved her and he happened to be Demeter's brother and lord of a mighty kingdom. Zeus also told her that in case she was totally-unwilling to let Hades have Persephone as his wife, he would let their daughter return to her as long as she had eaten no food in Hades' dark kingdom. But if she had already consumed the food of the dead, she was condemned to remain in the netherworld.

Demeter brusquely told Zeus that she would wait for her daughter to meet her on the meadow she was abducted from and till that happened the earth was condemned to remain barren and wells dry.

Zeus was very upset at the obstinacy of Demeter. He immediately despatched his son Hermes to Hades with instructions to bring Persephone back to her mother. Hermes set upon his mission and on reaching the underworld told his uncle Hades respectfully about the large-scale devastation upon earth caused by the angry goddess Demeter who would listen to no one from among the gods including Zeus. Hermes also told Hades about Demeter's grief at the abduction of her daughter which, he said, was beyond description and consolation.

Hades was quite understanding. He allowed Persephone to accompany Hermes to her mother. He reminded her that he loved her and promised to be a good husband to her. He also assured her that she would be respected, even worshipped, by the dead.

Persephone was pleased to hear Hades as he allowed her to visit earth, her mother, sunshine and flowery meadows of Sicily, and expressed love towards her. At the moment of her departure from the netherworld, her husband gave her a pomegranate seed deliberately so that Persephone could not remain forever upon earth. Persephone had eaten nothing upto that time. She swallowed the seed with a smile without suspecting any foul play.

Persephone returned to the meadows which, once ablaze with

Demeter, Goddess of farm-wealth and greenery on this earth.

beautiful colours of scented flowers, lay barren before her. As she alighted from the chariot of her brother Hermes, she threw her arms around her mother and embraced her happily.

Demeter was delighted to see her daughter. Since she was worried about her daughter's future, she instantly asked her if she had eaten anything in the kingdom of Hades. Persephone replied that it was only at the time of her departure that she had accepted a pomegranate seed from her husband. She said she had swallowed it because she was very hungry and also because she was unaware of the consequences of her action. Persephone was all in tears when her mother told her that her father and king of gods Zeus had decreed that if Persephone had partaken of any food in the kingdom of the dead, she was condemned to remain in the netherworld forever.

Just at that moment Rhea, the mother of gods including Demeter, reached the meadow. Rhea embraced her daughter Demeter and her grand-daughter Persephone and exhorted them to overcome their grief and face the destiny with courage and cheer. Rhea, then, delivered to them the message she had taken with her from Zeus, her son and king of gods, which said that they were welcome to Mount Olympus. The message also conveyed that Persephone was required to stay in the dark kingdom of her husband Hades for only one third part of the year and for the rest of the year she could happily stay with her mother on earth in sunshine and in the midst of flowery meadows. Persephone was allowed to leave the underworld at the dawn of spring and required to return there at the beginning of winter.

Rhea asked Demeter to put aside her anger against Zeus and be happy at the prospect of being together with her daughter for eight months during a year. She called upon her daughter to make the earth green again, let seeds grow and life return to earth. Demeter was glad to hear her mother's words. She agreed to bear separation from her daughter for a short duration of four months during a year and gladly let life return to earth causing the fertile land to bloom once again. Having settled the issue thus, Demeter returned to Mount Olympus and joined her brother and lover Zeus with whom she was no more angry. ■■

Roman Myths-1 : Apollo, Diana and Venus

The Greeks and the Romans had common gods and almost common myths. Mount Olympus was the seat of Gods for the Greeks as well as the Romans. According to legends and myths, it was Aeneas, the son of Venus, the goddess of beauty and love and her lover Anchises, who had brought culture and good government to Italy at the head of a large number of Trojans driven out by the invading Greek armies. Aeneas married Lavinia, daughter of the Latin king Latinus, after humbling his Latin rival Turnus who had long sought Lavinia in marriage.

In course of time Iulus, Aeneas' son, founded Alba Longa and it was his descendants who later built the city known as Rome. Anchises, the lover of Venus and father of Aeneas, took particular care to take Greek gods with him while leaving Troy, and these gods were later adopted by Romans as their gods.

But they changed the names of Roman gods. Zeus is Jupiter, his wife Hera is Juno, Hades is Pluto, Aphrodite is Venus, Artemis is Diana, but Apollo remains Apollo in Rome too. In Greece, Helios, the sun god had later become Apollo. For Romans, Apollo was the chief god, the giver of light and life, the great healer, patron of athletes, god of poetry and music, the inspiration for oracles, soothsayers and prophets.

Apollo : The Tragic Lover

Roman mythology presents Apollo as a tragic lover. He once fell in love with Casandra, the daughter of King Priam of Troy.Apollo was moved by her beauty and he was prepared to give her anything in return for her love. He bestowed upon the maiden the power of prophecy. Inspite of Apollo's best gift to Casandra, she refused to extend her love to him. Apollo was highly dejected. He could not withdraw his gift from her. So he cursed her that while she would be able to make true prophecies, she would not be trusted. Apollo's curse to Casandra ultimately brought ruin upon her father's kingdom and destroyed Troy. Casandra forecast Greek attack upon Troy but her people did not trust her. Accordingly, they made

Both the Greeks and the Romans have common Gods and myths, though the names of Gods differed.

Juno (Hera)

Jupitar (Zeus)

no preparations to face the Greeks and this resulted in their ultimate destruction.

Apollo's love was rejected by another beauty, Sibyl, who lived at Cumae on the western coast of Italy where Apollo had a temple. Apollo promised her any gift in return for her love. He met Sibyl at the sea-shore near a huge heap of sand. Sibyl was not willing to accept Apollo's love, but out of fun she playfully asked Apollo to let her live as many years as there were grains of sand in the heap. Apollo readily agreed. He then suggested that in case Sibyl was willing to marry him, he would also grant eternal youth to her so that she did not have to undergo the ravages of old age. Sibyl refused. She preferred to do without the gift of eternal youth rather than marry one whom she did not love.

Apollo then fell for Daphne, a graceful nymph, who had long been trying to discourage Apollo's advances since she realized that she could not return Apollo's love and affection. She was fleet-footed and whenever Apollo approached her, she ran as fast as she could. On one occasion, however, Apollo was determined to embrace her and he pursued her as fast as Daphne was running away from him. But just at the moment when Daphne was at an arm's distance from Apollo, a miracle happened. Apollo stood cheated and astounded to find Daphne changing into a laurel tree. The tree bark started encircling her and her arms changed into branches of the tree in no time. Then Daphne's beautiful hair turned into foliage.

Apollo, while pursuing Daphne, had heard her cry out in terrified accents. After she was converted into a laurel tree, Apollo realized that her cries were meant to invoke some vegetation divinity which had answered her prayer and had transformed her into a tree. Apollo helplessly broke down at his sweetheart being converted into wood, and he lovingly embraced the tree. He decreed that the laurel tree should be regarded as sacred and always associated with his name.

Marpessa was another young maiden who received Apollo's love, attention and favour. He offered her his best gifts, but the girl's heart lay in a mortal, Idas. Idas frankly admitted to her that being a mortal he could not compete with a god in offering her gifts, but he could humbly offer her his heart's best love and in this respect he could beat Apollo. Marpessa did not want to become the wife of the sun-god and live happily in the heavens. She preferred to marry a

Daphne, a graceful nymph, changing into a laurel tree when Apollo was chasing her.

mortal like her and live upon earth. Apollo was once again rejected. He was a tragic lover in the real sense as his own sister Diana had earlier refused to marry him. Instead of marrying him, Diana chose to remain unmarried.

Diana : The Huntress

Diana, who was Apollo's twin sister and daughter of Jupiter and his beloved Leto, was fond of wandering through forests and hunting stags. She was worshipped as protectoress of unmarried girls who looked to her for help in all their difficulties. At the time of marriage, young girls offered all their dolls and toys at the altar of Diana as a mark of their gratitude for her help and protection during their virginhood.

Diana was kind to girls who sought her help, but she was equally cruel to those who displeased her. Once when she was enjoying a cool bath in a jungle pool, a young hunter named Actaeon happened to pass through that way and quite inadvertently caught a glimpse of Diana. Diana noticed the act and got furious. As a goddess, she knew that Actaeon was innocent, yet she instantly converted him into a stag. Soon Actaeon's hounds saw the stag. Unable to realise that the stag was in fact their master, they began chasing him. Actaeon, the stag, fled in terror. He tried his best to call his dogs and to make them realise that he was their master but he failed. Finally, as he fell on ground exhausted, his own hounds tore him down. This was the height of Diana's cruelty.

Diana was unmarried but she was a great lover at the same time. She had become very fond of her hunting companion Orion. Diana and Orion had common tastes, so they became intimate friends. Apollo became suspicious of their closeness and looked for an opportunity to finish Orion. One day Apollo accompanied Diana and Orion to seashore. While Apollo and Diana were talking, Orion went into the sea for a swim. Apollo had been watching him, but Diana was quite unaware of Orion. Apollo decided to finish Orion on that occasion. He pointed a dark spot in the sea to Diana and challenged her to try her shooting skill on the object. Diana accepted the challenge and taking her bow in one hand shot an arrow which hit the dark spot. She never knew that she had shot the head of her best friend Orion. When she came to know of it, she was grieved to the core of her heart. To honour her friend, she raised him to heavens and installed Orion as a constellation.

Diana was also worshipped as the goddess of moon and addressed as Cynthia. Once she fell in love with a handsome young shepherd. Diana's father Jupiter did not want his daughter to fall for a mortal and that too a mere shepherd. He, therefore, told the boy Endymion that he had to choose between death and perpetual sleep. If Endymion chose perpetual sleep, he was offered perpetual youth too. Endymion opted for perpetual sleep.

Next time, when Diana saw Endymion sleeping during the night, he appeared extremely beautiful, his face glowing in full moonlight. Diana could not resist the temptation to kiss him. She really came down and kissed Endymion. Endymion is still in perpetual sleep and eternal youth. On every full moonlight, Diana descends from heavens, takes his head into her arms and kisses him

Diana, kissing Endymion when he was asleep.

with all her heart's passion. Diana, who had decided to remain unmarried, had actually become victim of the play of Venus, the goddess of love, who takes pleasure in arousing love in the hearts of gods as well as mortals.

Venus : The Love Goddess

Goddess Aphrodite of Greeks became Venus for Romans. Greeks held that she was born of the sea-foam, but the Romans believed that she was the daughter of Jupiter and the nymph Dione. Venus symbolizes love between male and female in the world of living beings--the force that reproduces life.

Venus was beauty incarnate and she possessed all the womanly charm and grace. It is really a matter of pity that the loveliest goddess at Mount Olympus was given to Vulcan-the ugliest among the gods, heavily built and lame-as his wife. Vulcan was a blacksmith by profession.

According to the Romans, Venus had a son, Cupid, who always attended upon her. He constantly carried with him his bow and arrows-some tipped with gold and others with lead. The former were used to make one fall in love and the latter produced exactly the opposite effect.

Venus had another son Aeneas who established his sway over Italy and whose descendants later established Rome. Venus was kind-hearted and she almost always helped lovers. Personally she had a number of love-affairs to her credit like other gods.

The king of Greece had a daughter Atlanta who was a swift runner. Her father had decided that he would give Atlanta in marriage to a young man who could outdistance her in a foot race and the competitor had either to win the race or lose his life. A number of Atlanta's suitors had laid down their lives in this manner. Once Atlanta saw a young man Hippomenes who looked at her somewhat scornfully as if he regarded it foolish of her suitors to risk their lives for the sake of a bride. But in fact he was deeply in love with Atlanta though she was not aware of it. Hippomenes had prayed to Venus to help him in winning the hand of Atlanta. Venus was kind to him. gave him three golden apples and instructed him in their use.

When Atlanta saw Hippomenes among the competitors, she felt disinclined to compete with him. By now she had developed a sort of kind disposition towards him as he had been successful in arousing a feeling of love in her heart.

The race began and Atlanta kept ahead of Hippomenes. After a little while, Hippomenes rolled one golden apple on the track in front of Atlanta in accordance with the instructions received by him from Venus, the goddess of love. Atlanta had to slow her pace a bit in order to pick the apple, but she was still ahead of Hippomenes and confident of winning the race. After they ran some more distance, Hippomenes rolled another golden apple on the track. Atlanta picked the second apple too, still ahead of competitors. Then, finally, Hippomenes rolled a third golden apple, but at some distance from the track this time. Atlanta thought for a moment about the risk involved in slowing down her pace in order to pick the third apple. Confident of her fleet-footedness, Atlanta took the chance and picked the third apple too. But this time she lost the race to Hippomenes who outdistanced her in the final lap. Atlanta, it is said, was struck by the handsome Hippomenes and she deliberately chose to slow down her pace under the pretence of picking the golden apples. They were happily married and throughout their wedded life offered sacrifice at the altar of Venus for they owed their union to her.

Statue Gains Life

Once Venus saw that a young artist Pygmalion had fallen in

Venus, with the handsome young shepherd Adonis

love with the statue of a woman he had made and named as Galatea. He sat for hours gazing at the statue and adoring it as if it were a living being. On the occasion of a festivity, Pygmalion loaded the altar of Venus with precious offerings and eatables. This pleased Venus highly, and she converted the Galatea statue into the Galatea woman-a living being. Pygmalion was astonished to notice the statue transformed into a living woman with far more beauty than he had put into it and looking at him with deep love and infatuation. Pygmalion could think of nothing except expressing his gratitude toward Venus, the goddess of love, before taking Galatea into his embrace.

Adonis

Venus was wedded to a bulky, ugly and lame god Vulcan while she herself was a beautiful goddess. She always sought love outside her marriage. She had a number of lovers, but she was most beholden to a handsome young shepherd Adonis who was killed in a combat with a wild boar. Venus was completely out of joint at her lover's death and she refused his dead body to be taken from her arms unless gods promised that he would live with her during spring and summer, and that she might stay with him for the rest of the year in the world of the dead.

Romans had special regard and fascination for Venus. They could never forget that it was under her guidance that her son Aeneas led the Trojan race to Italy. They raised high and beautiful temples to her. The founders of Rome--Romulus and Remus--were her descendants. They made Venus the presiding deity of Rome.

■■

Roman Myths - 2 : Romulus and Hercules

The Romans were pre-eminently warlike people. It was natural for them to have taken Mars as their patron god. They regarded Mars as their divine ancestor too, as he was believed to have sired the Roman heroes Romulus and Remus—the founders of Rome.

After Troy was destroyed by the Greeks, the Trojans who survived came to Italy under the leadership of Aeneas, son of Venus. Iulus, son of Aeneas, in course of time established the city of Alba Longa and made it his capital. One of the descendants of Iulus was Numitor who ruled over Alba Longa. Numitor had a brother named Amulius, who was highly jealous of his brother and wanted to become the ruler of Alba Longa in Numitor's place. After some time he succeeded in his mission and usurped the power from his brother's hands. In order to make his throne safe, he also tried to destroy Numitor's children lest they make a claim to the throne of Alba Longa. Numitor's son was killed by Amulius and his daughter Rhea Silvia was made a priestess of goddess Vesta obliging her to remain a virgin for the whole of her life.

But the gods willed otherwise. One of them, god Mars, fell in love with Rhea Silvia and made her pregnant. Rhea Silvia later gave birth to twins--Romulus and Remus. On hearing the news of the birth of twins to his niece, Amulius summoned her before him and charged her of immorality. Rhea Silvia's plea that she was made pregnant by Mars, a god, fell on deaf ears and she was thrown into prison. Her sons were snatched from her and packed in a wooden casket which was to be submerged in the waters of river Tiber. The river was flooded due to heavy rains and its waters had entered fields stretching upto the outskirts of the city. Amulius' men, charged with the task of consigning the casket to the river, thought it perfect to leave the casket in the river's overflowing waters and did so.

God Mars had never lost track of his sons. He observed the king's men leaving the casket containing the twins in the flood waters. He immediately asked Tiber to withdraw to its mainstream. Tiber responded to Mars' instructions and left the casket on the dry land.

By chance a hungry she-wolf, who was passing that way, saw the casket and tore it down with its sharp teeth. The she-wolf was first delighted to find her food in the form of twins, but the next moment her heart was filled with filial affection for the boys and her udders became heavy with milk. She immediately picked the boys by her jaw, took them to a lonely and secure place and sucked them on her breast. As the children grew, a bird, which had become very fond of them, provided them with further nourishment in the form of bread-crumbs which it brought in its beak from a distant place. The children began to grow in size and strength.

Mars thought it was the time for the children to be shifted to a human household to prevent them from becoming wolves in human form. One day a shepherd named Faustulus chanced to pass through the spot where the she-wolf was affectionately licking the twins. Faustulus was amazed at the sight. The she-wolf had never permitted any creature, except the little bird which fed them crumbs with her little beak, approach the children. But when Faustulus, motivated by the desire to take the children home and bring them up as his own, approached them, the she-wolf did not growl at him even once, nor did she resist his effort to lift the children in his arms. She behaved as if her mission was fulfilled. She watched Faustulus taking the children in his arms passively with sad eyes.

Faustulus brought Romulus and Remus home and handed them over to his wife, a barren woman, who was extremely delighted to see them and treated them as God's gift to her.

The shepherd and his good wife brought the children up. Romulus and Remus soon grew into two strong, courageous and well-behaved young boys. They spent most of their time on rearing the cattle, farming and hunting. When they came to know that the area was infested with robbers, Romulus and Remus collected a number of shepherd boys and began attacking robbers. They would kill them, recover their booty and restore it to its owners. It made them into popular heroes.

One day some robbers laid a trap for Romulus and Remus. Romulus fought back valiantly and was able to escape from their trap, but Remus could not. The robbers captured Remus and took him to king Amulius. They charged the twins of stealing cattle of the former king Numitor. Amulius, after hearing their charges, sent Remus to his deposed brother Numitor for punishment.

Meanwhile, Faustulus had, on the basis of the widespread rumour that Amulius had a casket containing two new-born babies consigned to Tiber river, become convinced that Romulus and Remus must be the twins. He had always suspected royal blood in their veins looking at their courage and love of justice, particularly manifest in their act of killing robbers and the restoration of the property looted by them to its rightful owners.

Faustulus thought it advisable to take Romulus into confidence on this issue and he did likewise. Numitor also knew that his brother Amulius had snatched his daughter's twins from her and despatched them to be drowned in Tiber waters. When the robbers took Remus to him and told him that he was one of the twins, the idea flashed into his mind that Remus might be his grandson. When questioned about his parents, Remus told Numitor that he regarded himself and his brother as sons of Faustulus. At the same time, Remus told him that he had heard rumours about their childhood, their exposure to flood waters of river Tiber and rescue by a she-wolf.

Numitor got convinced that Remus was none other than his grandson--son of his daughter Rhea Silvia. He asked Remus to contact his brother Romulus and aid them in building two separate armies of shepherds. According to the plan, the armies led by Romulus and Remus marched upon the palace of king Amulius from opposite directions and slayed him in a surprise attack. The people of Alba Longa were happy to be relieved of an oppressor and had Numitor restored to his throne as their king.

The two brothers then worked hard to found a city at the spot where men of Amulius had left them in a casket to drown. They built a beautiful city, but as they were equal in age, they did not know how to decide who should rule over the city. They tried to seek help of the local gods but it was of no avail as each one of them was determined to become ruler of the tiny state created by them jointly. They fell out and started raining blows on each other. Romulus struck a heavy blow at the temple of Remus killing him instantly.

Romulus gave the city his name and it has ever since been known as Rome. Romulus became the first king of Rome. He invited the poor and the slaves from neighbouring communities to settle in Rome with a view to increasing the city's population.

One of the major problems facing Romulus was acute shortage of women in Rome. He wanted neighbouring communities to marry some of their girls into Rome, but they would not. They did not want Rome to grow in population and consequently in strength. They also regarded Romans as inferior to them.

Romulus had a sharp mind. He decided to organize a great celebration in honour of god Neptune and invited his neighbours to grace the occasion with their presence along with their women and children. There was a sea of people surging towards Rome. They were all eager to see the new city about whose grandeur they had heard so much.

The celebrations started. When they were at their height, Romulus gave a predetermined signal to his city-folk, and they seized all of the visiting women in a split second. The unsuspecting guardians of the women were taken by surprise and outraged but they were quite helpless and defenceless. They had to return to their cities without their women. The women thus captured by Romans were given a personal assurance by Romulus that Romans would be good husbands to them and the ladies would have all the freedoms and privileges Romans had. Romulus warned Roman men that anyone who misbehaved with his wife would be deprived of one and reduced to the status of a slave liable to be assigned to his former wife's new household. The women kept their trust in Romulus and lived in Rome serving their men faithfully. But their relatives from the neighbouring communities failed to reconcile with the situation imposed upon them by Romulus. They kept making armed raids on Rome from time to time and Romulus had hard time defending Rome. It were the women themselves who finally decided to face their relatives and they forced them to come to terms with Rome, their new home.

Romulus had a mysterious end. One day when he was reviewing a military parade surrounded by his senators, a violent storm rose in the sky and a dark cloud enveloped him. Everybody ran for shelter but Romulus was in the firm grip of the cloud. After the storm blew over and the sky cleared, there was no trace of Romulus to be found. His people believed that he had been called to heavens and made a god. They built him a shrine and worshipped him as one of their gods.

Hercules

Romans held Hercules as one of their mythological heroes like Greeks who called him Heracles. He was the son of Jupiter from a distinguished woman named Alcmene, though he was commonly known as the son of Amphitryon, the husband of Alcmene.

Jupiter's wife Juno hated Hercules and wanted him dead. She would never agree to Hercules being raised as a god by her husband. So she prescribed twelve trying feats to be performed by Hercules to qualify as a god.

One of these feats was killing of Hydra, the awful nine-headed monster which infested the Lernean swamp not far from Argos. Hydra used to roam about in the nearby countryside, lift oxen and devour them making it difficult for farmers to cultivate their fields.

Hydra's middle serpent-head was immortal and no one from among gods or men had been able to slay it. Hercules shot blazing

Hercules, killing the nine-headed dreaded monester Hydra

arrows at it and forced it out of the swamp. Then he grabbed Hydra's middle head with his hand and started smashing its other heads with his club. It was a fierce fight reminding one of Lord Krishna's fight against the Kaliya Naag (Dark Dragon) in the swamps of the holy river Yamuna near Vrindavana.

Hercules started smashing Hydra's heads, but as soon as he did it, other heads grew in their places. He then directed his companion to put a log of wood into burning fire and sear the bleeding necks with the burning log as soon as Hercules cut them off. This device prevented Hydra from growing new heads. Hercules chopped off Hydra's immortal middle head and buried it under a huge rock. Then he cut Hydra's trunk into pieces and dipped his arrows into Hydra's blood in order to make them deadly. ■■

Myths of Japan - 1 : Gods

Japan is an ancient land rich in mythological lore and legends. It has its own mythology of creation of the universe, the gods and human beings. In the beginning, according to Japanese mythology, there was a primeval oily ocean mass out of which a reedlike substance emerged. This became the first deity. At that time heaven and earth were shapeless mass. In course of time, the lighter part became heaven and the denser, heavier part became earth. Earth, in the beginning, was a muddy mass devoid of the force of gravitation. It, therefore, floated in the space between the heaven and the oily ocean.

The first deity--the reed--kept floating in a state of weightlessness after its emergence. At the same time, with the emergence of the reed deity, two other divine beings appeared. Japanese mythology does not say much about them except that they reproduced and several generations of gods and goddesses came into being. The first gods identified by the Japanese mythology are Izanagi and Izanami, male and female respectively. They were born in the heaven, the abode of gods, and they descended down to the oily ocean mass by a bridge commonly understood as rainbow. The brother asked the sister if she could see any firm land-mass below. Izanami could perceive nothing but liquid all around. At this Izanagi suggested that they would better take the heavenly jewel-spear into their hands and thrust it into the ocean. In case there existed any solid land mass, the spear would automatically reveal it. Then they held the spear in their hands jointly and dipped it into oily mass. The spear revealed no land. But as they pulled the spear from the ocean, the drops of the oily mass that dripped upon the ocean surface coagulated by themselves and formed the first muddy substance. Izanagi and Izanami brought this muddy substance together and created the first land mass, the island of Ono-koro.

Once an island was created on the surface of the ocean, Izanagi and Izanami left the rainbow and descended upon it. They built a beautiful palace on the island and placed the heavenly spear in its

Izanagi and Izanami, the first male and female on this earth, watching a pair of wagtails making love.

centre as its main pillar. After doing that, they got married to each other. Though they lived together as husband and wife, they did not know anything about the art of love-making. One day Izanagi and Izanami stood at the seashore watching a pair of wagtails making love. The scene aroused conjugal feelings in their heart and taught them the art of love-making. They then produced eight lovely children, each of whom became an island and it were these eight islands that formed Japan.

Once the land was created, Izanagi and Izanami produced the gods of wind, mountains, valleys, forests, streams of water, green meadows and trees. Then, at the insistence of Izanagi, his wife gave birth to the goddess of sun as the ruler of the universe named Amaterasu. She was the most beautiful and bright among their children, so they asked her to ascend to the heaven and shine from there over the entire universe created by her parents. Izanami then gave birth to the god of moon, a beautiful and brilliant though calm child. He too was sent to heaven ascending the bridge, the rainbow, to become the husband of Amaterasu, the sun-goddess.

Izanagi and Izanami then had another child named Susano. They loved him a lot, and perhaps it was their love which spoilt Susano. From his childhood he had destructive propensities, yet his parents gave him earth to rule over. But when they saw that he was the most unworthy ruler and a merciless god, they banished him to the underworld called Izumo and named him as Izumo's ruler. He was also designated as the god of storm.

Finally Izanami gave birth to the god of fire. In the process of his birth much heat was generated in Izanami's body. She had burning fever which finally killed her. According to another version of the myth, god of fire was born to Izanami after she gave birth to eight islands, and after his birth she expired. The other gods Amaterasu, the moon-god and Susano, the storm god, were born to Izanagi from his eyes after the death of his wife Izanami.

Still another version of the myth says that while dying Izanami gave birth to the goddess of earth and the goddess of water. The goddess of earth was taken by the god of fire as his wife and gave birth to a daughter who produced the mulberry tree and the silkworm from the hair on her head and five kinds of grains from her navel.

Izanami's Death

After leaving her body Izanami went to dwell in Yomi, the netherworld. It is easy for the dead to leave the living and proceed to Yomi (Yama Loka--world of the dead), but those who are left behind find it difficult to bear the separation. It was much more difficult for Izanagi because his entire world was limited to Izanami who had been with him since birth. He had created the universe together with Izanami. The concept of eternal separation from her was quite foreign to him. He was born of gods and he had never seen people dying. So death of Izanami became unbearable to him and he pursued her to Yomi. On seeing Izanami in the underworld he told her that he would have to take her back with him as he could not live without her.

At this Izanami protested and told him that it was impossible for her to leave Yomi as she had already eaten Yomi's food. She also told him not to shed light upon her and to go back to the world of the living as death had ended the marriage between them. Izanagi would not. Contrary to Izanami's instructions, he lighted a candle to see her in the dark chambers of Yomi and was disgusted to see the rotting corpse of Izanami.

Izanami was now furious upon Izanagi. She called eight ugly witches of Yomi and ordered them to chase Izanagi out of Yomi. At the end of the tunnel, separating the land of the sun and land of Yomi, Izanami threatened Izanagi that if he did not leave her alone, she would strangle 1000 of his subjects every day. To this Izanagi replied that he cared not a hoot about that and that he would create 1500 people daily.

Then Izanami gave up anger and begged of Izanagi to forget her as her time on earth was over. She advised him to reconcile with the concept of death, separation and ending of marriage and return to his people and live there peacefully. She asked him to wait till the end of his life on earth, and she told him that he could join her on his death if he remained a true and loving husband to her till that day.

Izanagi, following the advice of his dear wife, returned to earth. He remained true to her till the end of his life and never for a moment thought of another woman as his wife. Izanami and Izanagi were once again united in Yomi after the death of Izanagi.

Amaterasu

Amaterasu, the sun goddess and ruler of the universe, was living in the heaven with her younger brother and husband, the moon god, happily and she created mortal living beings on earth. Amaterasu then appointed Uke-mochi as deity of food on earth in order to feed the human beings and take care of their welfare. Some time later she sent the moon-god down to earth to find out how the food deity Uke-mochi was doing her work.

In order to entertain the moon-god, when Uke-mochi opened her mouth facing the land, boiled rice streamed from it. Next she turned her face toward sea and fish and sea-weed were regurgitated. Finally she faced the wooded hills and the game of various kinds came forth.

Uke-mochi then gathered and cooked all these and served repast on 100 tables for the moon-god to feast upon. But the moon-god, who had seen how the food-deity had spit the food articles from

Amaterasu, the sun goddess and ruler of the universe.

her mouth, was disgusted at the sight of food which he thought had been made foul by her. This thought made him furious. He felt slighted by a lesser deity and became so violent that he killed her with his sword and rushed back to heaven. He straightaway went to Amaterasu, his wife, and narrated the incident before her in the minutest detail.

Amaterasu was enraged to hear her husband. She scolded him vehemently and told him that she could no longer stand sight of his face. Since that day they have never met face to face. They live apart from each other. According to Japanese mythology, the sun and the moon have an uneasy relationship and sit in their celestial abodes with their backs to each other; hence the day and the night.

After divorcing her husband, Amaterasu despatched the cloud spirit as her messenger to earth to find out the conditions there after the death of the food-deity. The cloud spirit reported back to her that even in death Uke-mochi's body continued its work. Cows and horses issued forth from her head, silkworms from her eyebrows, millet grew from her forehead and a rice plant sprang from her stomach. The cloud spirit had collected these products which he presented before the sun goddess. Amaterasu was pleased with Uke-mochi finding that she did her duty to the last, and she exclaimed that human race would be highly benefited by those articles of food, clothing and animals. The cows would provide them with milk and oxen to plough their fields, and they would be able to use horses as the beast of burden.

Amaterasu appointed a heavenly village-chief on earth and entrusted him with the responsibility of sowing and growing the various seeds in appropriate seasons. She kept in silkworms in her mouth and collected silk yarn from them. Later she asked the silkworms to be left to grow upon mulberry trees produced by the daughter of the goddess of earth and the god of fire. Amaterasu taught human race the art of preparing silk thread and making cloth from it.

Once Amaterasu saw Susano, the storm god, approaching her celestial domain. She knew that Susano was a troublesome brother and he could try to harm her in order to snatch the authority over heavens and earth from her hands. She, therefore, made preparations to face him in the event of his attack upon her. But Susano assured her that his intentions were peaceful and he simply wanted to visit her before going down to the dark world entrusted to him by their father Izanagi. Amaterasu let him stay with her happily. But soon she found that Susano had destroyed her rice fields, had defiled the purity of her palace on the occasion of the harvest-feast and, when she had set weaving silk cloth for gods, he had removed roof tiles and thrown a colt into the hall which had startled her so badly that she had pricked her hand with the shuttle of the loom.

This was the last straw on the proverbial camel's back. Amaterasu could no more tolerate Susano. She, therefore, shut herself in the rock cave of heaven, causing darkness on earth day and night. Human beings and gods alike were badly upset, but no one knew what to do about it. After some time they decided to place a statue of the sun goddess at the gate of the rock-cave and worship her. The worship started, and gods and goddesses sang and danced in her praise day and night. Amaterasu became curious about the celebrations outside her cave and, opening the door of the cave a little, peeped from the opening. As soon as the gods saw her doing that, they held her by hand and led her to celebrations and requested her to accept the offerings they had brought with them for her. The gods also punished Susano and marched him to his kingdom in the neth-

Izanagi and Izanami, searching for solid mass of land with jewel-spear

erlands. Amaterasu was thus pleased with the gods and human beings, accepted their offerings and resumed her charge of the universe.

Amaterasu decided to make her grandson Ninigi the ruler of the Japanese archipelago created by Izanagi and Izanami. She gave him the regalia of royalty: the sword, the mirror, and the jewels. Ninigi was a celestial ruler, not a human emperor. Ninigi fell in love with Ko-no-hana, daughter of Oho-yama, possessor of the great mountain. They were subsequently married and Ko-no-hana gave birth to two sons. Ninigi's younger son married the sea king's daughter who gave birth to a son and returned to the sea. But she sent her sister to look after her child. The child reached manhood and married his aunt who had brought him up. In course of time, they produced a son Jimmu Tenno who became the first emperor of Japan. ■■

Myths of Japan - 2 : Benten and Butterfly

In Japanese mythology Benten, the goddess of sea, occupies a special place among the gods and goddesses of luck. She is the goddess of literature and music as well as the giver of wealth and fulfilment in love. She is regarded as the daughter of the dragon king of the sea. She is also believed to have married a dragon who used to devour children in the village near his abode. After his marriage with Benten, the dragon lost appetite for human flesh.

Benten is depicted as the goddess of mercy seated on a lotus flower in the lotus posture. She has eight hands. She employs a white serpent as her messenger. Once a young man Baishu went to offer his prayers to Benten for a happy marriage at her shrine in the Amadera temple. There he saw a newly created pool of water and a new temple dedicated exclusively to goddess Benten. Baishu entered the new temple to offer his prayers and, as soon as he was seated before the deity, a piece of paper came floating in the air and settled near his feet. Baishu lifted the paper in his hand, and lo! it was a love poem inscribed in a female hand.

Baishu took the paper with him and studied it minutely. Finally, he decided to marry the girl who had inscribed the poem in her hand, and he went back to pray at the shrine of Benten in the Amadera temple compound. He prayed to the goddess to reveal the identity of the girl to him and assist him in securing her hand. He vowed to pray daily at the shrine for seven days and spend the night of the seventh day in vigil.

A little before dawn on the eighth day, when his vigil was about to be over, an old man entered the shrine followed by a young man. The young man prayed to the old man that the time had come to bring about the union for which the prayers had been said so sincerely. The old man remained utterly silent. He took out a red cord from the sleeve of his shirt and tied one end of it around Baishu who stood amazed. The other end of the cord was put by the old man into the flame of one of the lamps of the temple. He was moving the

Benten, goddess of mercy, sitting on a lotus flower in the lotus posture.

burning end in the air and before the fire could reach Baishu, a young woman entered the shrine and took her seat beside Baishu. The cord was then removed.

The young man, who had asked the old man to help in the union, now spoke to Baishu and told him that his prayer was granted by Benten. He added that it was at the orders of Benten that the old man had invoked the girl who had written the love poem on the paper that had settled at Baishu's feet. After a while Baishu found that he was alone in the temple and all others who had appeared, including the girl introduced to him as the writer of the love-poem, had disappeared. They were all apparitions. Apparition of the girl met him again as he neared home on his way back from the temple. She lived with him for a number of months as his wife, but no one except Baishu could see her because she was invisible to others. She was an apparition.

At the beginning of the winter Baishu went out for a stroll and reached a spot he had never been to before. It was there a man approached him and told him that his master wanted to see him. The servant and his master were complete strangers to Baishu. Still Baishu went in to see the servant's master who told him that he knew Baishu as his would-be son-in-law. The gentleman also told him that it was he who scattered love poems written by his daughter in order to find her a suitable husband. He had prayed to Benton; and Benton told him in his dream that a suitable husband had been found for his daughter who would visit him quite soon. Benten visited him again on the previous night and told him that his daughter's future husband would pass near his house on the following day. Benten had also given him detailed description of the young man, so he did not find it difficult to identify Baishu.

At this point Baishu wanted to tell the man that he was already married, but the man slid open the door connecting the adjoining room. Inside the room Baishu saw the young woman who had already been living with him in his house and had been accepted by him as his wife in the temple.

Baishu was now wedded to the young lady as arranged by her father. The only strange thing about the whole affair was that Baishu's wife made no mention of meeting, marrying or living with him previously. This was because earlier she had known him and been with him in her ethereal or spiritual form. It was so willed by goddess Benten because she wanted to test Baishu's love for the young woman, and when she was sure that Baishu would make a loving husband to the girl, she instructed her father to give his daughter to Baishu in an earthly marriage.

The Butterfly

In Baishu's case the spirit of her beloved visited him while she was still living. Here is a Japanese myth which speaks of the spirit of a lady who expired before her marriage to her beloved man, and which visited him after her death till he breathed his last.

There lived a rare type of man who had never had any relations with a woman for fifty years and who was nearing 70 years of age. At this age, the man fell sick. He had no one to look to but his brother's widow who was living at a distant place along with her son. He thought of this lady and informed her about his illness. The lady felt strongly for her brother-in-law and came to his place with her son to be with him during his illness and looked after him.

Akiko and her beloved.

One day the old man was lying in his bed with his young nephew by his bedside. Suddenly the young boy saw a large white butterfly enter the room through a window and hover upon his sick uncle's bed. The butterfly would stop for a while, rest on the sick man's pillow and then again flutter about him. After a short while, the boy saw the butterfly fly straight out of the window.

The butterfly aroused curiosity in the young boy's mind. He got up from his seat and followed the butterfly. He found it flying in the direction of the local cemetery just across the road from the house of his uncle. The butterfly then disappeared into a grave which was recently tended and had a stone carrying the name Akiko.

The boy returned to his uncle's bedside only to discover that the old man had died. He was shocked at his uncle's death. Then he got busy with the formalities in respect of his funeral, church service, family mourning and so on. Later, when calm returned to house, he spoke about the entire episode to his mother: visit of the white butterfly to his uncle, his chase of it and its disappearance in a recently tended grave in the cemetery across the road. His mother then told him that as a young man his uncle was in deep love with a girl named Akiko. They were betrothed but Akiko died just before the day their marriage was to be held. Akiko was buried in the cemetery across the road and he (her brother-in-law) bought the house he was living in at the time of his death with a view to be near her grave which he took care of for almost 50 years. He never once mentioned the subject to any one during the half century of mourning he was observing.

The boy's mother was sure that the white butterfly was none else than the spirit of Akiko which had come to fetch the spirit of the man she loved at the close of her mundane life and who loved her throughout his life exclusively and faithfully. ■■

Iceland Myths - 1 : Thor's Hammer

Myths of Iceland are the myths of Northern Europe recorded primarily in Iceland in the 13th century A.D. Norse myths portrary gods possessing human personalities and imbued with human motives and emotions. They are subject to the unalterable destiny and death, very much like human beings. They prefer to die as heroes. Norse myths speak of a perennial state of war between gods and demons like the Indian mythology, but contrary to Indian mythological practice the Norse myths end in defeat of gods at the hands of giants. The ruler of gods, Odin, is aware of the fate of gods but he is helpless in its face; he has no power over giants.

Odin is the supreme Norse god. Goddess Frigg is his wife and Thor, the god of lightning and thunder, is their son. The abode of gods is known as Asgard, the abode of human beings (earth) as Midgard, and the abode of giants is Jotunheim.

Besides Thor, the supreme god Odin and his wife Frigg have four more sons--Baldur, Hodur, Hermod and Bragi. Idun is Bragi's wife. She keeps the golden apples of eternal youth which she serves to gods in order to keep them young. Norse has a god of fertility and ruler of the winds and the sea--Njord. Njord has a son, Frey, and a daughter Freya. Frey is ruler of the sun and the rain-god while Freya is mother goddess and is a consultant on matters of love. Gods of Iceland have a watchman, Heimdall, and a mischief-mongering and trouble-shooting god Loki who is the son of two giants. Loki has a monstrous daughter named Hel who rules over the dead in the netherworld called Niflheim.

Norse myths speak of frost giants like Thjazi and Thrym who reside in Jotunheim. Thrym is in love with mother goddess Freya and to obtain her hand he steals the chief weapon of Thor--the divine hammer named Mjollnir—which brings ruin upon him and his people.

The Hammer is Missing

Thor is the superman in the Norse mythology. One morning

Odin, the supreme god of Northern Europe

Thor found that his chief weapon Mjollnir, the hammer, was missing. He searched for it here and there and when he failed to locate it he got enraged and desperate. He immediately contacted Loki, the mischief-monger and trouble-shooter of gods, and told him about the missing hammer. Loki knew where it could have been taken and who could have stolen it from Thor. He assured Thor that he would do his best to recover his hammer in the shortest possible time. Loki took Thor with him to Freya's abode and asked her to lend him her falcon-feathered cloak so that he could fly to Jotunheim to search for Thor's mighty weapon. He told her that he was almost sure that it must have been stolen by a giant alone as no one else could have dared to touch it.

Freya readily agreed to lend him her cloak and Loki, having put the cloak on, flew to the world of giants, Jotunheim, where he noticed the Frost Giant Thrym in the Hall of Giants. Thrym looked at Loki and asked him about the gods and mischievous fairies. Loki explained to him how gods and elves were upset because of the theft of Thor's hammer Mjollnir.

Thrym confessed to Loki that it was he who had stolen Thor's

Thor, the superman of Norse mythology, flying in his chariot at the wind speed with Mjollnir (the hammer) in hand.

hammer and buried it very deep in the earth. Thrym also told Loki that he was willing to return the hammer to gods provided goddess Freya, the grand-daughter of Odin and Frigg, was willing to marry him. In no other way could gods get it back from him.

Loki again put on the falcon-feathered cloak lent to him by Freya and arrived at Asgard in no time flying back at the wind speed. He was met by Thor as soon as he landed. Thor anxiously asked him if he had been able to locate his hammer.

Loki narrated to him what Thrym had told him. On hearing that he could get his hammer back only if Freya married Thrym, he accompanied Loki to Freya's palace. Thor could not think of engaging Thrym in a fight for two reasons: first, his chief weapon hammer had already been stolen by Thrym rendering him helpless; and second, Thor knew it very well that the giants were much more powerful than the ease-loving gods of Asgard and it was out of question to defeat the giants and force them to surrender his hammer. The only course open before the gods was to persuade Freya to accept Thrym as her husband.

Freya reacted to this proposal of Loki angrily. She was already married to Odr,and she was not at all willing to be disloyal to him and take a giant as her husband instead.

Thor was satisfied with Freya's reply. He went straight to the supreme god Odin. Odin immediately convened an emergency conclave of gods to deliberate and decide upon the vital issue of the recovery of Thor's hammer in the absence of which gods were left without defence. Amongst the gods, Heimdall was the wisest. He advised the assembly to enter into a conspiracy in order to cheat Thrym and kill him fraudulently. He suggested that Thor should be thoroughly dressed up as a bride and his face hidden behind a bridal veil. Thor shirked at the idea but Loki and Heimdall ultimately succeeded in bringing him round. Thor was made to wear the best of Freya's robes and jewellery that covered him from top to toe. His face was covered under a bridal veil. Loki was to accompany Thor to Jotunheim. He was made up as Freya's handmaid. Thor, then, traversed the skies in his chariot and arrived at Thrym's palace-ground to be welcomed and received by Thrym and his fellow giants.

The sun was about to set. Thrym first offered his would-be

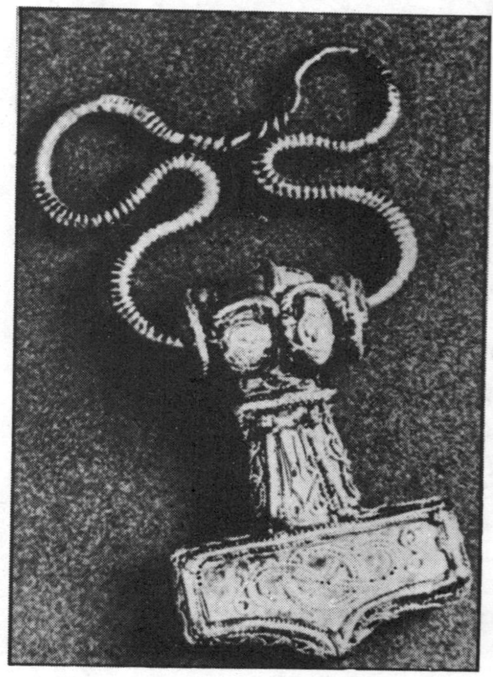

The missing divine hammer of Thor, later recovered from Thrym.

bride with sumptuous meal and jars of ale. Thor, who was disguised as Freya, consumed all the food served on the table, a whole ox, a large number of salmon and a large quantity of ale. Thor could not resist the temptation of eating quite forgetting that he was acting as a decoy. Thrym and his fellow giants were dismayed at his bride's appetite. Loki, disguised as Freya's handmaid, sensed the mood of Thrym and in order to save the situation told Thrym that Freya was so anxiously waiting for her wedding with him that she could eat nothing for eight days. Thrym was moved to hear Loki. He lifted the veil and leaned forward to kiss his bride but he was terrified to see the burning eyes of Thor. Loki once again craftily handled the ugly situation with the remark that Freya could not go to sleep for eight nights as she was anxiously waiting to meet her bridegroom.

Thrym was convinced of Freya's love for him. He ordered the hammer of Thor to be placed upon the bride's lap as a mark of good omen and heavenly blessing. His fellow giants complied with his instructions immediately and it was now Thor's turn to act. Thor was extremely happy to see his mighty weapon upon his lap. He quickly held it in his hand and smashed Thrym's head instantly. He killed Thrym's fellow giants too and returned to Asgard with his hammer in his hand and Loki by his side upon his chariot. It was a rare occasion when gods had scored a victory over giants in Norse mythology though it was made possible only through intrigue and fraud. Probably the gods thought that it was not possible for them to score a victory in an open trial of strength and that is why they took recourse to intrigue and fraud. ■■

Iceland Myths - 2 : Idun's Apples

Once upon a time a giant Thjazi ruled over Jotunheim, the land of giants. Thjazi knew that the secret of the eternal youth of gods lay in Idun's apples. Idun, wife of Bragi, one of the sons of Odin and Frigg, had a basket of golden apples. Idun used to feed the apples to gods which kept them in vigour and perpetual youth, and it was because of her divine and magical powers that her basket would neither go empty nor fall short of supply. Thjazi, therefore, decided to have Idun brought to his kingdom. He remained in search of an appropriate occasion to achieve his objective in order to secure eternal youth for the giants.

Once Odin, Loki and another god Hoenir left Asgard on a journey northward without taking any food with them. As they reached the valley down the hills, they saw a herd of oxen and realized all of a sudden that they were hungry. The gods picked a healthy oxen out of the herd, slaughtered the animal, lit a fire and roasted it till it was brown. They sat down to eat the meat, but to their surprise they found that the meat was raw. They relit the fire and roasted the meat again. They sat down to eat it after it had turned brown this time. Again they realized that the meat was raw despite its colour. Odin was puzzled at the riddle. He asked his companions as to what should have prevented the meat from being roasted. His companions could think of nothing, but a voice from the skies revealed that something sitting upon the oak tree beside them prevented the meat from being cooked.

The gods looked up and saw the giant Thjazi sitting upon one of the branches of the oak tree in the form of a huge eagle. Loki, on behalf of the gods, asked the eagle why it was preventing the meat from being cooked. The eagle replied that it would allow it to be cooked only after having as much of the oxen meat as it liked. The gods agreed and the eagle took away a large chunk of it. This enraged Loki and he struck the eagle with the stick he was holding in his hand. But the stick got stuck to the eagle's body and the eagle flew into the sky with Loki trailing behind it holding the stick in his hand. Loki found that he was unable to leave the stick. The eagle flew low over the hill so that Loki's feet crashed over the mountain surface. Loki was badly injured and he began to fear that his arms were soon going to be pulled out of the shoulder sockets. He, therefore, requested the eagle in an humble tone to let him go before he was finished.

The eagle told Loki that he would let him go provided he promised him to bring Idun along with her basket of golden apples to him. Loki had no option before him but to give the eagle the promise it had asked for to save his life. He swore to keep the promise, and the eagle let him go.

Loki returned to the valley from where he was abducted by the eagle, but he did not tell Odin about the condition on which the eagle had let him go. The gods returned to Asgard. After a few days Loki told Idun that he had seen some beautiful apples in the valley. He invited her to accompany him to the valley along with her basket of golden apples so that she could compare the apples in the valley with her own apples and if she found them in order she could add them to her collection.

Idun had no reason to disbelieve Loki. She was thrilled at the prospect of finding some more golden apples to add to her basket and she set out for the valley with Loki. As they reached the valley, Thjazi appeared before them in the form of a huge eagle. Before Idun could realize the gravity of the situation, it picked her in its claws and flew away with her.

Loki returned to Asgard alone. Gods at Asgard soon realized that Idun had disappeared. They searched for her here and there. Loki joined them in the search appearing quite innocent. Idun's disappearance was not an ordinary affair for the gods. They owed their perpetual youth to Idun's apples, in the absence of which their bodies began to betray signs of old age and decay.

An upset Odin called the assembly of gods to meet and discuss the problem. Some one from among the gods revealed that before Idun disappeared, he had seen Loki leading her away from Asgard. This was enough of a clue for the gods to grab Loki and threaten him with death in case he failed to bring Idun back to Asgard.

Loki promised the gods to look for her in Jotunheim. He asked

Idun, captured by Thjazi because of her basket of golden apples.

Freya to lend him her falcon-cloak so that he could fly to Jotunheim. Freya gave him her cloak and Loki immediately flew to Jotunheim.

On reaching Thjazi's home, he found Idun alone in the house as the giant was out rowing upon the sea. Loki transformed Idun and her basket of golden apples into a small nut which he held firmly in his hands and flew back hurriedly toward Asgard. But he was not out of danger. After a little while Thjazi returned home to find Idun missing. He immediately assumed the form of an eagle and rose into the sky where he saw a falcon flying in the direction of Asgard. Thjazi recognized the falcon and chased it.

Loki had by this time reached so close to Asgard that gods could see him followed by an eagle in the sky. The gods immediately realized that Loki was being pursued by Thjazi. In order to prevent Thjazi overtake Loki, they placed bags of wood shavings around the walls of Asgard fort and as soon as Loki flew over the wall into Asgard, the gods set the shaving bags ablaze. Within a few moments, flames began to leap into sky. Thjazi saw the flames but he was flying at such a tremendous speed that it was impossible for it to change its course. It flew into the flames and fell to the ground at the Asgard gates to be killed by gods.

After the news of Thjazi's murder by gods reached the ears of

Skadi, the daughter of Thjazi, she put on her coat of armour and taking weapons in both the hands reached Asgard to avenge her father's death. She was met there by Odin, the supreme god, who told her that according to the custom she was entitled to compensation for the life of her father. She, therefore, could choose one of the gods as her husband on the basis of his feet.

Skadi accepted Odin's offer. She was already in love with Baldur, Odin's son. Baldur was a handsome young man and so, she thought, his feet must be. Thus she chose the most beautiful feet which turned out to be Njord's.

Her failure to choose Baldur as her husband made her sad. Her sadness created a problem for gods because according to the custom it was incumbent upon them to have the recipient of the compensation laughing. Odin told her that their payment will not be deemed sufficient unless they made her laugh. Skadi refused to laugh as she was not happy at her choice of husband. But Loki ultimately succeeded in making Skadi laugh at his antics. Then, in order to please Skadi, the supreme god Odin took out Thjazi's eye balls with his own hand and tossed them into the heavens to become bright stars. At this honour granted to her father by the father of gods, Skadi was thoroughly reconciled with the gods. Thereafter, she lived at Asgard with her husband Njord happily. ■■

Myth of Canada : Raven

Along the western coast of Canada live the culturally rich Indians who inhabited among animals and birds in ancient times. The Haida tribes developed a close relationship with these creatures. This is best revealed in the Raven myth which explains how Raven, the mighty and intelligent celestial being with powerful wings of a bird, secured release of the sun and placed it in the heavens to relieve the Haidas from the evil effects of darkness.

The universe had just been created and the sun had already been placed by the creators in the heavens when the Haida people were given a chief to look after them. The chief lived near the source of the Nass River. He was a selfish man and he had no love for his people. Out of his greed for light, he captured the sun, the moon and the stars and kept them so securely hidden from his people that no one knew about their whereabouts.

In the absence of the sun, the earth refused to bring forth the vegetation and in the absence of the moon, the Haida people could not catch fish at night. For want of food, the Haidas lived a miserable life. Close to the Haida settlement and on the banks of Nass River there lived Raven, a celestial bird with mighty wings and a kind heart, which seethed at the sufferings of the inhabitants of the universe--human beings and other creatures alike.

Raven had heard that the sun, the moon and the stars had been imprisoned by the Haida chief. He, therefore, decided to visit the chief and secure release of the sun, the moon and the stars. He knew that to reach the chief's village, he had to fly a long distance over the Nass River. So he collected a number of pebbles in his bag and set upon his flight. Whenever Raven felt tired, he dropped a pebble into the river. The pebble immediately formed into an island for Raven to alight upon and rest for a while.

Finally Raven arrived at the Haida chief's village and sat thinking about the best mode of entering the chief's house to secure release of the light. After a while, Raven saw the chief's daughter with pitchers. She filled the pitchers with water and before leaving the river bank she washed her hands and face and drank the river water heartily.

Raven observed the girl's behaviour closely and decided upon the course for him to adopt. He waited at the river bank for full one day. The chief's daughter visited the place again. Raven transformed himself into a small seed. When the girl picked the water into her palms, Raven the seed concealed himself between her fingers and as she drank the water he slipped into her mouth stealthily. Raven the seed travelled in the inside of the chief's daughter cautiously, and lodged himself safely into her womb.

The chief's daughter became pregnant. In due course of time, she delivered a son. The boy was Raven in disguise. The chief became very fond of the boy. He played with him and gave him all his heart's love and everything that he demanded for playing.

The boy began to crawl. One day he saw a number of bags hanging on the walls of his grandfather's house. He started weeping and would not stop until the chief promised to give him anything he wanted. The boy pointed towards the bags. The old man rolled the bags on the floor for the child to play with. The boy peeped into the bags and found stars stored in one of the bags. He took that bag into his hands and let it go. The bag suddenly lifted upwards and escaped through the opening in the ceiling meant for smoke. The bag flew higher into the sky and spilled the stars into the space.

The chief was sorry at the loss of whatever little light the stars could provide him with but he was not prepared to displease his grandson. When on the next day, the boy started crying, the chief gladly rolled the bag containing moon on the floor for the boy to play with. The boy played with the bag and giggled. The chief was happy to see his favourite grandson enjoying. After a while the boy rolled the bag on the floor at the spot exactly below the chimney and let the bag go off. The bag lifted up, passed through the opening and rose straight into the sky where it burst open and released the moon into the space.

The chief was pained at the loss of moon too, but he did not suspect his grandson of foul play. The time went by and the boy continued to play with bag after bag and box after box, but he did not release any other bag or box into the sky.

One day the child saw a huge box and he would not stop crying

Raven, the mighty and intelligent with powerful wings, savior of the sun, the moon and the stars.

unless his grandfather opened it. But the chief was cautious this time as he was not prepared to lose his most precious possession stored in the box. He, therefore, covered the smoke-vent in the ceiling of the house and opened the box for the child with instructions to take care of his grandfather's dearest and most precious possession.

From inside the box the chief took out another box, tightly sealed with spider's web. There was a third box inside the second box and then the fourth one until the chief had eight boxes in his hands. With great hesitation, the chief opened this box and from it emerged a ball of light--bright, brilliant light. It was a fiery ball.

The boy demanded the ball to play with and the chief gave it to him. The boy was delighted to have it. He would play with it and leave it after some time perhaps getting tired. The chief would then repack the fiery ball in the boxes.

The boy was waiting for his opportunity to release the fiery ball into the sky as he knew it was nothing else but the sun. As days passed, the chief became more and more relaxed and less and less careful about closing the smoke-vent in the ceiling of the house which could not be kept closed all the time. It had to be uncovered for smoke to pass through it. The chief had so many things to do. He would give the sun to the boy and let him play with it all alone in the house.

One day the boy discovered that he was quite alone in the

house and the smoke-vent was open. He immediately transformed himself into his Raven form, held the sun firmly in his claws and flew through the smoke-vent into the sky.

Raven wanted to have a little play with the Haidas. As he flew over the river, he saw some people catching fish under the cover of darkness. Raven alighted on a tree top and said to the fishermen that if they promised to share their catch with him, he would give them some light. The fishermen did not trust him. But when Raven revealed the sun from under his wings, the fishermen gave him fish enough to fill his belly.

The practice continued for a few days. Then feeling ashamed of his greed and selfishness, he lifted his wings, tossed the sun into the sky with his claws and exclaimed happily, "Let my people have light both during day and night." Since then Raven has been guarding the sun, the moon and the stars in the sky and no one had the courage to steal them. ■■

Myth of Mexico : The Maya Gods

The Maya civilization, located in Guatemala and the Yucatan peninsula of Mexico in Central America, was one of the richest civilizations of the ancient world. It originated 6,000 years before the advent of Christ and lasted till 1524 A.D.,when the Spaniards from Europe destroyed it. Maya culture is very rich in its mythological lore. The Mayans were great astronomers and they built temples atop huge pyramids in which they worshipped their gods. Sun was their chief deity; and rain god Chac another important god to appease whom the Mayans sacrificed virgins in a cenote or the sacrificial well in the Chichen Itza temple complex in Yucatan. The Mayan gods also, like the gods in other myths, wanted to create human beings. The kind of human beings they created in the process has amply been manifested in one of their myths.

In the beginning there was neither air, nor fire. There was a state of total calm and quiet. The earth was covered by a vast sheet of water and there was sky overhead. There was no third element. Life was not yet created, but Gods existed. They lived under the sheet of water, covered by green and blue feathers. They were highly intelligent beings and they discussed between themselves the manner in which earth could be raised from water and all pervading darkness overcome.

One day the gods announced their decision to begin creation. They defined their task as filling the void, withdrawal of sea to a reasonable limit allowing the earth to emerge and creation of light. They invoked the earth to rise up and fulfill their ambition. The earth arose, the sea receded and beautiful forests grew on the rich soil of the hills that had emerged out of sea.

The gods assembled again and after expressing satisfaction over their creation, they labelled it as perfect. But the basic question before them was : would they like the silence to continue or would they create life around the trees, on the hills and in the marshy plains? They decided to create birds, animals and snakes.

The gods assigned those creatures grounds to rest and to move

Perhaps this structure with sky-facing architrave used to be the Mayans' ceremonial offering-place to the celestial Gods

about, and trees to build nests. They also endowed them with the faculty of speech or sound, and asked them to cry, chirp, hiss and call the gods by name and shower their love and praise upon them. But the animals, birds and snakes could not praise the gods as their sounds were not clear enough.

The gods then decided to create a superior race of living beings who would rule over the animals, birds and snakes and kill them for food. The goods expected the new specie to praise and love them. Ultimately, they created the new genre of living beings out of mud, but the model was not satisfactory as the material out of which they were created was too soft to be enduring, the language they spoke was quite unintelligible and they were also incapable of procreation. The gods, therefore, destroyed them and created a new model out of wood. Wood proved to be a firm and strong medium, and the new creatures looked and spoke like human beings. The model was approved and the gods engaged in creation of the new specie of living beings. But the worst thing about them was that their faces were wooden and therefore expressionless, and they had no soul, no blood and no lov for the gods who had created them.

Two of the many Mayan deities.

Ultimately gods decided to destroy the wooden beings forthwith. Those creatures put up a tough resistance but most of them perished and those who remained alive had their faces badly deshaped. They became the forefathers of monkeys.

The gods were in search of some new material from which they could shape human beings of their concept. One day four animals appeared before gods and led them to a nearby place where yellow and white ears of corn grew abundantly. They gathered the corn, ground it and from its flour fashioned four superior creatures. The gods prepared corn meals and corn drinks and gave that stuff to the four human beings as food. As a result, the model human beings began to grow in strength and wisdom. The gods then declared that they were duly satisfied with the human beings that they were finally able to produce. They called the human race their perfect creation.

Gods waited to see whether the four model human beings they had fashioned and approved praised and loved them. The four forefathers of mankind were highly intelligent and wise people. They had the power to visualize all that existed within the universe-beyond the skies and beneath the earth, the mountains, the valleys and the sea. They were amazed at what they saw, and their hearts

A Mayan Temple in pyramid shape.

were full of praise and love for the great gods who had created the universe. They were grateful to the gods for having fashioned them and endowed them with the faculties of seeing, hearing, speaking, thinking, feeling, walking and discriminating between good and bad, right and wrong.

The gods were pleased to find the model human beings offering their gratitude, praise and love to them. But they also apprehended, perhaps that the models had become better than they intended them to be and any such possibility they did not like to come across. So the gods blew fog into the eyes of the four model human beings in order to limit their vision and their farsightedness.

Thus the gods finally approved the model human beings who duly became the forefathers of the human race. Then the gods created four women and supplied one to each of the men, while asleep, as their wives. The gods created more human couples who procreated in large numbers under the cover of darkness that en-

Mayan rain-God Chac

veloped the earth. They lived in the east. Some of them were light-skinned and others dark-skinned, some were rich and others were poor. But all of them prayed to the gods for progeny and for light.

The gods granted their prayers and created the sun, the moon and the stars. The eternal darkness ended, and one fine morning the sun rose from the waters and cast its golden rays upon the earth. The entire creation was overjoyed to see the dawn.

It was a sight worth witnessing-animals, snakes, birds and men all gathered under shades of trees and on river banks. The animals filled the skies with their wild roar, the birds sang melodious songs in praise of the gods, the snakes hissed and human beings prayed, sang and danced to express their gratitude and love towards gods. Priests burned incense and offered sacrifices to gods. They all celebrated the first illumination of the universe.

The temples built by the Mayans stand upto this day with large pots of incense waiting for the priests to be burnt, but the descendants of the Mayans have vanished into oblivion, perhaps because their gods wished it that way. ■■

Myth of Africa : Mwindo

Mwindo is the epic hero of the Nyanga tribe in the Zaire state of Africa. Mwindo is a moral hero and the sphere of his conquests includes all the three regions--the earth, the heaven and the netherworld. He teaches his people to respect all forms of life and give equal consideration to the young and the old, the male and the female and the sick and the healthy..

King Forbids Male Child

Once upon a time there was a Nyanga tribal chief named Shemwindo. He had seven wives. He decreed in public that his wives were allowed to procreate only daughters,and if any one of them gave birth to a male child,the child would be killed and the wife who bears him would be abandoned by him.

The chief's seventh wife Nyamwindo became pregnant and when delivery was due, the child in her womb would not leave it. Nyamwindo's belly was getting larger day by-day-and she was getting frustrated. Another disturbing feature was the occurrence of strange events. One day Nyamwindo saw a bundle of firewood placed at her door. Another day she found a jar full of water inside her house, and fresh vegetables on the third day. She failed to realize that it was the child she was carrying who helped her in her daily chores.

Finally, her trial came to an end. She gave birth to a son who despised a normal course of delivery. He was born from the middle finger of his mother's right hand. The strangest thing about him was that as soon as he was born he began talking to his mother, and he was born with a sceptre in his right and an axe in the left hand. He was extremely handsome and his face glowed like the moon and the sun. He also carried with him a bag of fortune containing a long miraculous rope slung over his shoulder.

The child was named Mwindo--the first born male. The midwife and the nurses did not want to announce the birth of the child for they knew that the Chief would slay the child and abandon

Nyamwindo. But the news could not be concealed from the Chief as a cricket, which was present in the chamber where Mwindo was born, went to Shemwindo and broke the news to him. Shemwindo was enraged to hear that the nurses had concealed the news from him. He took a spear in his hand and hurried to Nyamwindo's quarters. As he stood outside the birth-chamber of his son, he heard his son's voice cry out from inside the chamber: "May my father's spear miss the nurses, my mother and myself. Let it strike the ground and sink into it."

Shemwindo was amazed at his son's power. He made six attempts to aim his spear at Mwindo, but instead of striking Mwindo, it would strike the ground again and again. Defeated and frustrated, he decreed his son to be buried in a deep grave. After the child was thrown into the grave and the Chief's men were about to seal the grave, they heard the child's voice calling: "Oh, my father, after you have suffered great sorrow, you will die like this."

Shemwindo was informed about the curse hurled upon him by his son. He realized the enormity of his son's power and thinking that if he survives he might dethrone him, he ordered his men to seal the grave tight. Alas, all his attempts were of no avail. On the night of his burial, Mwindo came out of the grave and went into his mother's quarters where he began crying,like a new born baby. The Chief heard the cries and stealthily went into Nyamwindo's chambers,only to find the child back in his mother's arms.

Next day Shemwindo ordered the child to be sealed in a wooden drum and left it in the mid-current of a nearby river so that it sinks to its bottom. The order was faithfully executed. But after seven days of incessant rains, when a group of village girls gathered at the river bank with their pitchers, they saw the drum floating upon the river surface and heard Mwindo's voice hurling curses upon his father and his counsellors. The terrified maidens rushed back to the village and informed the Chief about the return of Mwindo. Shemwindo personally visited the river bank where he saw the floating drum and heard Mwindo repeat his curse. As the Chief stood there dazed, the drum containing his son sank of itself to the river-bed.

After his father and his men returned to their places, Mwindo left the drum and swam to his aunt's place who lived upstream. The guard posted at the gates of his aunt Iyangura's house by her husband Mukiti stopped Mwindo from entering the house. Mwindo was adamant. He dived into the river and dug a tunnel leading upto his aunt's chambers. In this way, despite the barriers created by Mukiti and the village elder, Mwindo succeeded in reaching his aunt who welcomed him heartily. Now the village elder invoked the thunder god to kill Mwindo. Mwindo merely waved his sceptre and the thunder god struck at the village elder's head whose hair went afire. The villagers ran in search of water to put the fire out, but not a drop was left in their pitchers or in the tank of Mukiti. Seeing the village elder's miserable plight, Mwindo's aunt called upon him to withdraw his curse and let the fire leave the village elder. Mwindo waved his sceptre and the fire vanished,and water returned to pitchers as well as Mukiti's tanks. The villagers hailed Mwindo and he vowed to take his revenge upon his father

Mwindo Avenged

Accompanied by his aunt and her companions Mwindo went to see his uncles who were metalsmiths. They prepared for him an invincible armour and went along with him to his father's place to witness the battle between Mwindo and his father. His aunt continuously kept telling him that Shemwindo was very powerful and he would cut Mwindo into pieces, but Mwindo never bothered about it. Then there was the problem of food and shelter for all those who had joined Mwindo on his journey to his father's capital. By sheer will Mwindo created a row of houses with plentiful supplies of food and other essential articles for all of them.

Mwindo sent his uncles to destroy his father's people but they failed to harm them and died in the battlefield. Having entrusted his bag of fortune and magical rope to his aunt, Mwindo entered his father's village and invoked the thunder god to strike against his father and his people. The thunder god struck the village seven times. The village was completely ruined and Mwindo's father ran through an opening in the ground to the netherworld, the land of Master Muisa.

Mwindo brought his aunt to the village, touched his uncles with his sceptre and after bringing them back to life he took one end of the magical rope into his hand from his aunt and left for the netherworld in search of his father. He told his aunt that the moment the rope stops moving she should take him for dead. A sparrow which had seen Mwindo's father enter the netherworld flew ahead of Mwindo showing him the way.

In the netherworld Mwindo met Master Muisa and asked him to return his father to him. Master Muisa told Mwindo that if he succeeded in planting a new banana grove for him and make it bear fruit instantly, he would hand over Shemwindo to him. Mwindo raised the banana grove and made it bear fruit the next day, but Master Muisa went back upon his word and tried to kill Mwindo. Since Mwindo was invincible, he survived all attempts on his life and killed Master Muisa. Mwindo was successful in locating his father. While leaving the land of darkness, he revived Master Muisa with his sceptre so that he might rule over his domain as per divine arrangement.

Peace Restored

Mwindo brought his father back to earth. Then he restored all those to life who had perished because of his curse. Life returned exactly to the state in which it happened to be at the moment of destruction. Within three days Mwindo restored the whole village to normalcy.

Shemwindo was reconciled with his son. He gave a feast on the ninth day of the event. The entire village population assembled on that occasion at one place. Shemwindo, Mwindo and his aunt Iyangura appeared before the people and Mwindo asked his father to explain to the assembly why he had ill-treated him. Shemwindo admitted his mistake. He told the assembly that his consciousness was clouded by dark thoughts. He promised that in future he would respect male children and honour them equally with female children.

Iyangura also condemned the manner in which Shemwindo had treated his male offspring. She praised Mwindo for restoring life to his father and the villagers. Then it was Mwindo's turn to address the village assembly. He told the assembly that he no more entertained anger or hatred for his father. Whatever they did to each other was a thing of the past. Mwindo hoped that his father would be able to care well for his people and live in peace with himself.

Shemwindo was moved to hear the sentiments expressed by his son. He stood up and told his people that though it was not necessary for a Chief to express regret and shame for his actions before his son and his tribe, still he felt obliged to admit his guilt and shame publicly. Shemwindo also expressed his desire to abdicate and make Mwindo Chief of the tribe.

Mwindo asked his father to take his chair, and told him that during his lifetime he would never take his place, and if he did so he would be dead.

Mwindo's ideas were endorsed by the Chief's counsellors. They proposed division of the country between the father and the son to which Shemwindo readily agreed. Mwindo was made Chief of his father's village and Shemwindo moved to another village to be its Chief.

A Just Ruler

Mwindo was a just ruler. Immediately on becoming the Chief of his village, he announced that he would acknowledge and respect all other family groups besides his own and welcome birth of numerous children--male as well as female, handicapped as well as healthy. He wanted all the villagers treated on an equal footing.

After a few days Mwindo came to know about a dragon which had seven heads, seven horns and seven eyes in the nearby jungle. The dragon had swallowed three hunters who had killed a wild pig for Mwindo. The fourth hunter had escaped and taken the news to Mwindo. The new Chief decided to do away with the dragon. Shemwindo tried to dissuade Mwindo from embarking upon such a risky mission as the dragon was very powerful and extraordinarily large. Mwindo would not listen. He went into the jungle and after a grim fight with the dragon succeeded in slaying him. The dragon's belly was slashed and the villagers were amazed to see the three hunters the dragon had devoured the other day coming out alive from its belly.

Mwindo asked his people to consume the monster to the bones. The villagers gathered at the centre of the village and started cooking the dragon's organs. They were surprised to find human beings emerging from the drops of the liquid that flowed out of the dragons eyes. From all the seven eyes a total of 1000 people had emerged. Mwindo welcomed these people and provided them with houses to live and land to till.

Mwindo's trials were not yet over. The dragon was a close friend of the thunder god who was enraged at his friend's killing by Mwindo. The thunder god visited Mwindo and challenged him to have a duel with him. Mwindo agreed. He rose above the clouds and defeated the thunder god instantly. Then the thunder god decided to let Mwindo prove his might against other gods of the space, and he challenged Mwindo to engage in a trial of strength against rain god, moon god, sun god and star god. Mwindo remained in the space for full one year and won appreciation of all the space gods. He was escorted back to his village by the thunder god.

Mwindo was instructed by the star-god to refrain from killing animals and insects whether in his village, in the forest or in the rivers. After his return to his village, Mwindo assembled his people and told them that he had been forbidden to kill. He narrated before them his heroic feats. He told them that it was good to be a hero but it was equally important to be forgiving and kind. The greatest of heroes was destined to meet one day a greater hero who had the power to destroy him. The worldly power is never absolute; it is always relative and so it would be foolish on one's part to believe in one's invincibility.

Mwindo helped his people in building good houses for themselves, growing multifarious and richer crops and making the village beautiful and clean. He advised his people to eschew disagreement, anger and hatred among themselves, to agree with one another, to refrain from the pursuit of another's wife or husband, to accept all their children whether male or female, tall or short, healthy or handicapped. He wanted them to be good to the sick even if they are strangers. He laid down that one who seduces another's spouse shall be slaughtered. He promised to accept, fear and protect his people and taught them to accept, fear and protect their chief.

Mwindo soon became beloved of his people and he was respected far and wide for his wisdom and love of justice. ■■